AMAZING GRACE

AMAZING
GRACE

JIMMY SWAGGART

JIMMY SWAGGART MINISTRIES
P.O. Box 262550 | Baton Rouge, Louisiana 70826-2550
www.jsm.org

ISBN 978-1-941403-45-7

09-158 | COPYRIGHT © 2018 Jimmy Swaggart Ministries®

20 21 22 23 24 25 26 27 28 29 / Sheridan / 11 10 9 8 7 6 5 4 3 2

DEDICATION

In what I remember to be the very first book I ever wrote, I dedicated it to Frances: "Who has been more than a helper. Her faith in God and confidence in me has been my foundation." Those words still ring true, only they mean a great deal more to me now, which is why I carried them here, and set them up front where they belong—at the beginning of our story.

TABLE OF CONTENTS

AMAZING GRACE

FOREWORD

FOREWORD

IT'S AN HONOR FOR me to write the foreword of Dad's book about his life and his ministry. It's fitting, I suppose, that I write it because aside from Mother, I'm the only one who truly knows what it was like all those years to observe, live with, and learn from this extraordinary man of God, who also happens to be my father.

I'm 64 years old, and Dad has been in ministry all of my life. I grew up watching him do the work of God, which really amounts to building faith in others. Some people believe *in* God. My dad *believes God.*

Anyone in full-time ministry can testify as to how demanding and draining it can be. For the five-fold gifts, ministry life is one of constant motion, especially, I believe, for the evangelist.

In the mid-1950s, when Dad started, most people saw the job of evangelist as a traveler who moved, physically, from one meeting to the next, spreading the good news. And that's what Dad did—he went from small church to small church to small church. But he soon learned that the God-called evangelist never arrives at his destination because the harvest stretches out continually before him, like miles and miles of open road. His only source for direction comes from time spent with the Lord, as does his message for the people.

I've said before that as a boy, I always knew that my dad was different. I couldn't describe then exactly how he was different; it was more of something I sensed. But all these years later, I can say with surety that the "something" I sensed was God setting my Dad apart—apart from other men, other preachers, even other Bible scholars. As Christians, we are all called to separation, but those who are chosen—they must follow God to the desert, alone.

Few will ever know the personal cost of that journey.

Throughout my Dad's ministry, I have seen him loved, and I have seen him hated, simply for the word that the Lord gave him to preach. It's not easy to stand by and watch sinners and saints alike publicly attack your parent. Human instinct is to hit back; a son's desire is to protect. Many times, I would have gladly taken Dad's place, to spare him. But deep down, I knew that God was with Dad—just as He was with Moses, and with David, and with Paul—no matter how many critics were against him.

That brings to mind President Theodore Roosevelt's famous words:

> It is not the critic who counts; not the man who points out how the strong man stumbles, or where the doer of deeds could have done them better. The credit belongs to the man who is actually in the arena, whose face is marred by dust and sweat and blood; who strives valiantly; who errs, who comes short again and again, because there is no effort without error and shortcoming; but who does actually strive

to do the deeds; who knows great enthusiasms, the great devotions; who spends himself in a worthy cause; who at the best knows in the end the triumph of high achievement, and who at the worst, if he fails, at least fails while daring greatly, so that his place shall never be with those cold and timid souls who neither know victory nor defeat.

When I think of Dad and his days in ministry—from preaching in the tiniest churches to standing before tens of thousands in the world's coliseums—the experience is comparable, in my mind, to that of a soldier's. The Army private who advances, over many years, to the rank of general.

In both cases, such promotions are rare. Each requires a lifetime of service above self and a willingness to lay down one's life, daily, for the cause.

But unlike the highly decorated officer, the preacher wears no ribbons or medals for the spiritual battles he's fought. No citations record his courageous faith, nor his many war wounds suffered for the brethren. Nevertheless, the scars are there. Men who wrestle with God come away with a limp.

I know my Dad, and he will never take credit for anything accomplished under the banner of Jimmy Swaggart Ministries. All of the glory, he says, belongs to the Lord. All of it.

Glory to God. No one says those words quite like Jimmy Swaggart.

I love you, Dad.

Donnie Swaggart

AMAZING GRACE

PREFACE

PREFACE

THERE HAVE BEEN ANY number of people who have requested that I write an autobiography of my person and this ministry; however, I have never felt led of the Lord to do so until recent days. But yet, I would not call it an autobiography simply because I have felt led of the Lord to deal only with the moving and the operation of the Holy Spirit within my heart and life. This has led to amazing things, for which we give the Lord all the praise and all the glory.

As we go through page after page, we will find that little by little the Holy Spirit is leading us to the Cross. This great revelation given to us is not new; it was given to the apostle Paul many centuries ago.

Yet, in about the third century, the early church began to lose its way, and this great message was ultimately lost, along with justification by faith, the grace of God, the mighty baptism with the Holy Spirit, etc.

So, what the Lord has given us is not new, but yet, it has not been known for centuries—back to approximately the third century. So, the great Message of the Cross will color our thinking, even when we do not understand this great word. However, most assuredly, the Holy Spirit gradually led us step-by-step to this—the greatest truth that believers can ever know:

- Jesus Christ is the new covenant.
- The Cross of Christ is the meaning of the new covenant.
- That meaning was given to us by the apostle Paul in his 14 epistles.

George MacLeod said:

I simply argue that the cross should be raised at the center of the marketplace as well as on the steeple of the church. I am recovering the claim that Jesus was not crucified in a cathedral between two candles; but on a cross between two thieves—on the town's garbage heap; at a crossroad so cosmopolitan they had to write His title in Hebrew, and Latin, and Greek ... At the kind of place where cynics talk smut, and thieves curse, and soldiers gamble. Because that is where He died, and that is what He died about. That is where the churchmen ought to be and what churchmen ought to be about.

I will close this introduction with a verse from a particular song, which I believe greatly epitomizes what I'm trying to say in this book.

These words that I will give to you were written by a particular pastor at whose church Frances and I had just closed a meeting. He was writing a short thank you note and quoted this song.

I don't guess I'll ever forget that moment. I sensed the presence of God so powerfully that day of long ago as I read these words. Instantly, the tears began to flow because they proclaimed my testimony, as they have, no doubt, done the same for untold millions.

————⟡————

I can see far down the mountain,
Where I have wandered many years,
Often hindered on my journey
By the ghosts of doubts and fears;
Broken vows and disappointments
Thickly strewn along the way,
But the Spirit (the Divine Spirit) led unerring,
To the land I hold today.

AMAZING
GRACE

THE HAND OF
THE LORD

"Whatever it is that God calls us to do, it is always beyond what we would, at first, see or think."

THE HAND OF THE LORD

THE LORD IS OMNIPOTENT, meaning *all-powerful*; omniscient, meaning *all-knowing*; and omnipresent, meaning *everywhere*. He notes every sparrow's fall and actually numbers the hairs on our heads each and every day. This is power and knowledge unimaginable. I firmly believe that in His omniscience, the Lord causes things to come to pass because of that which He knows will take place in the distant future. I think the illustrations that I will give bear that out.

A REVENUE AGENT

My parents, W.L. and Minnie Bell Swaggart, were married in the heart of the Great Depression of the 1930s. Work was almost nonexistent, and there was no government safety net. People had to somehow earn a few dollars to put food on the table, or they simply went hungry.

Both my mother and dad were born into homes that did not know God. In fact, my dad was 25 years old before he ever saw a Bible, before he ever heard a single gospel song, and before he ever darkened the door of a church. According to my mother's own words, she had only been to a couple of funerals in a church, and that was the extent of her spiritual knowledge. Consequently, I was born into a home that did not know God. And yet, I think the illustrations that I am about to give you will portray the hand of the Lord working so beautifully on behalf of that which would someday be, but definitely was not at the time.

MIRACLE OF MIRACLES

Even before my parents gave their hearts to Christ, there was never a drop of alcohol of any nature in our house. However, due to the fact that this was the time of Prohibition, meaning that it was against the law to make and sell alcohol in any fashion, still, millions of gallons were being brewed each day all over the nation.

At this particular time, my dad (along with Jerry Lee Lewis' dad) was making what was referred to then as bootleg whiskey. As stated, my mother and dad did not drink at all, but to put food on the table, they were involved in this unlawful activity.

It was in the month of February, about a month before I was to be born (on March 15, 1935). All of a sudden and without warning, revenue agents descended upon this group of men making bootleg liquor. The agents had sawed-off shotguns in the crooks of their arms, and those shotguns were leveled at my dad and all the others who were there. As they were putting the handcuffs on these men, the revenue agent who was standing closest to my dad looked over at my mother, who was eight months pregnant with me.

He asked my dad, "Is this your wife?"

My dad nodded in the affirmative.

That agent said nothing but slowly looked around and then said, "Son, I hate to put you in prison seeing that your wife is expecting a baby." He then said, "Is this your first one?"

My dad was only about 19 years old, and my mother was 18. The agent stood there for a few moments and then said, "Son, I'm going to turn my back, and if you're still here when I turn back around, you're going to prison, so I would advise you to vacate these premises as quickly as possible."

If my dad and my mother had been trying out for the Olympics that day, I think they would have surely made the team.

I've often wondered who that revenue agent was and what prompted him to let my dad go when all the others went to prison.

It has crossed my mind many times as to what would have happened to us had my dad gone to prison. Would we have found Christ?

Of course, I do not know the answer to these questions, but I do know this: I believe with all of my heart that it was the Lord who moved upon that agent for him to do what he did. I believe it was because of that which the Lord knew would take place several years from that day.

I don't know if that revenue agent knew anything about the Lord or not, but this I do know: If he is in glory when the Lord calls me home, I want to thank him for what transpired that day. As stated, it all started even before I was born.

TWO YEARS OLD

Once again we see the hand of the Lord in operation, which portrays the omniscience of the Lord.

Trying to put food on the table, my mother and dad went to a particular place where they could pick cotton. I think they were earning approximately 75 cents per 100 pounds of cotton. Of course, I was with them, but yet, I was only 2 years old.

My parents and I were staying in a little cabin, with other people staying in other cabins nearby.

At about midnight, my dad had a vision, even though he did not know at all what a vision was. In the vision, he saw me on the floor playing with some little toys that I had there. With it being in the dead of night, he rose up in the bed and called out, "Jimmy, what are you doing? Get back in bed." He said it two or three times rather loudly, but the truth is, I was not on the floor; I was in the bed sound asleep.

The next morning, my dad learned that someone had broken into each cabin on either side of where my parents were staying and had robbed and murdered the occupants. They found, as well, that the lock on the door to our cabin was almost disjointed. In other words, it was my dad's shouting at me that had stopped those murderers from coming in. They, no doubt, would have killed both my parents and me.

Now at the time, my mother and dad did not know the Lord whatsoever. However, the Lord knew that about three years later, they would give their hearts to Christ, and so He intervened at that time to save the lives of my parents and my life also.

Pure and simple, it was the Lord who engineered that scenario. At that time, my dad didn't know what a vision was, but that's what he had, and it was all supplied by the Lord.

SALVATION

The mother of Lester Sumrall and his sister had felt in their hearts that the Lord wanted them to go build a church in Mobile, Alabama; however, when they arrived there, every door was closed. They sat down on the bed in their little hotel room, spread out a map, and asked the Lord to show them where He wanted them to go to plant a church. He pointed out Ferriday, Louisiana. They didn't know where Ferriday was and didn't know anyone there, but every time they tried to get away from it, the Holy Spirit brought them back. Of course, the Lord knew what would transpire as a result of the church that was built there.

A few days after the Lord had given direction, Mother Sumrall and her daughter came to Ferriday. They secured permission from a particular individual who owned a lot where the church would begin. Once again, the Lord orchestrated events in a beautiful way.

One morning my Uncle Lee (in whose home I was born) was in his pickup truck, and he saw these two women trying to clear the lot with their bare hands. My uncle was a millionaire many times over and was possibly the richest man in the parish. He owned thousands of acres of land, owned hundreds of head of cattle, and had oil wells and gas wells on his property. He was very well-to-do, but to look at him, it seemed as if he were in poverty. I never saw him in a suit of clothes in my life, until he was buried. His wife was my mother's older sister, and, as stated, I was born in his home.

He rounded the curve and saw these two women trying to clear the lot with their bare hands. He stopped, walked out to where they were, and asked what they were doing.

They told him that they were going to stretch a tent, start a revival, and, prayerfully, erect a church. He looked at these two women, and they looked at him, never dreaming that they were looking at the richest man in the parish.

"Who sent you?" he asked.

Mother Sumrall stood tall—all 5 feet 2 inches of her—and said, "God sent us."

He listened to that, not really understanding what he was hearing, and then asked if they had any money. Their answer was, "God will provide." Well, He had already started providing.

That tent was stretched, people began to come, and souls began to be saved. The tall and short of the story is that my uncle loaned the money for that church to be built.

In those days my mother and dad were playing music for dances every weekend, trying to bring in a few dollars. One of my dad's closest friends, a man who was also an excellent fiddle player, asked my dad to bring his fiddle and come to church and join the church orchestra. Now, the orchestra consisted of an old upright piano, someone who played a rhythm guitar, and Pop Watson, my dad's friend, who played a violin.

My dad took his fiddle, along with my mother and me, to the first church service he had ever attended in his life. I may only be imagining it, but it seems as if I can remember that particular night. I would have been 4 years old, so it's doubtful that I can remember it, but it seems as though there is a smidgen of what took place indwelling in my mind.

At any rate, my mother and dad walked into that church—the first service they had ever attended in their lives—and Pop Watson told my dad to follow him to the platform, which he did.

Once again, and I may be wrong on this, but it seems to me that the very first song that they sang that night was the following:

I've found a friend in Jesus, He's everything to me,
He's the fairest of ten thousand to my soul;
The Lily of the Valley, in Him alone I see
All I need to cleanse and make me fully whole.

He'll never, never leave me, nor yet forsake me here,
While I live by faith and do His blessed will;
A wall of fire about me, I've nothing now to fear,
From His manna He my hungry soul shall fill.

Then the chorus:

In sorrow He's my comfort, in trouble He's my stay;
He tells me every care on Him to roll.
He's the Lily of the Valley, the Bright and Morning Star,
He's the fairest of ten thousand to my soul.

Strangely enough, even though the Lord dealt with my parents severely at that time, they would not say yes to Christ.

Coming up in the Depression, my dad wanted to make money. He was afraid that some of the things he might do would not be in keeping with the Word of God, so he held back.

RIO HONDO, TEXAS

My mother and dad got it in their minds that if they left Ferriday and went to South Texas then my dad could start a produce business and make a lot of money. I was 5 years old at the time. Strangely enough (I can remember this), when we left that morning, my mother and dad were singing a little chorus they had learned in church:

I know the Lord will make a way for me,
I know the Lord will make a way for me,
If I live a holy life, shun the wrong and do the right,
I know the Lord will make a way for me.

My mother was holding in her arms my little baby brother, Donnie, who was only 3 months old.

Yes, the Lord would make a way. My mother and dad thought they were going to Texas to start a business, but, in reality, they were running from the Lord. They were to find out that everywhere they went, the Lord was there.

Almost immediately after arriving in South Texas, my mother and my baby brother came down with pneumonia. This was in the days before penicillin, so this particular disease was fatal almost all of the time.

Actually, when my dad was getting a prescription filled for my baby brother, the druggist looked at it, looked at the doctor's name, and then looked up at my dad and stated, "You don't have anything to worry about. This doctor has never lost a case of pneumonia."

But what that druggist didn't realize was that the Lord had just spoken to my dad and said, "I'm going to take your son."

It was a night or two later when there was a knock at the motel room door. My dad opened it, and my uncle was standing there. Dad looked at him (I still see this in my mind), and he said, "It's Donnie, isn't it?"

My uncle dropped his head and began to weep, and he finally said, "Yes. He passed away about an hour ago."

I still see that little motel room. I see my dad weeping. My mother was also in the hospital with pneumonia, but, thankfully, the Lord spared her.

The next scene that comes to my mind is the burial service. I see the small graveyard and the casket that was opened. I looked down at my baby brother with his head of black curls, whereas mine was totally blonde. Then I heard my dad speak.

As he looked down at that little one in the casket, he said, "Donnie, I promise you one thing: by the grace of God, I will meet you in heaven."

A few days later, my parents went back to Ferriday, Louisiana, and to that little church.

If I'm not mistaken, at that particular time, Tom Holcomb was the pastor. He was the brother of Jack Holcomb, one of the greatest tenors in the world of that day.

I remember the night that my mother and dad stepped out and said yes to Christ. They had to pay a terrible price before they finally buckled, but it was a night that would change their lives forever, and it would change mine as well.

All that thrills my soul is Jesus;
Every day and every hour;
Jesus and His free salvation,
Jesus and His mighty power.

He is love beyond all knowledge,
His is grace beyond degree,
Mercy higher than the heavens,
Deeper than the deepest sea.

Every need His hand supplieth,
Every good in Him I see,
And the strength He gives His weak ones
Is sufficient to me.

What a wonderful redemption!
Never can a mortal know
How my sin though red like crimson,
Can be whiter than the snow.

And yon while in everlasting city,
With the ransomed I will sing,
And forever and forever,
Praise and glorify the King.

All that thrills my soul is Jesus,
He is more than life to me,
And the fairest of ten thousand,
In my blessed Lord I see.

AMAZING GRACE

CHAPTER 2

SALVATION AT EIGHT YEARS OLD

"Everything seemed different
after that day in front of the
Arcade Theater."

SALVATION AT EIGHT YEARS OLD

"I GOT SAVED."

That's what I told my mother that Saturday afternoon when I arrived home earlier than she was expecting me.

"Why are you home this early, Jimmy?" she asked.

Every Saturday afternoon I would go to the movies to see the cowboys, etc., but this day, I did not go.

As it regards church, I don't really remember anything before this particular Saturday. I was 8 years old. It was 1943, and it must have been in the summer months because I don't remember being in school at that time.

As stated, I don't really recall anything about church before that time, and yet, we were in every single service. We didn't miss any, irrespective of the weather, etc. If the church doors were open, my mother and dad felt they had to be there.

Our house was situated about a quarter of a mile away from the main road. Whereas there is a two-lane highway there now, then there were only mud ruts.

I can remember that when it looked as if it would rain, my parents would park the pickup truck that my dad had on the main road and walk to the house. When we went to church, and it was raining, we did the same thing. We didn't miss. However, as I've just stated, I don't have any recollection of the services or anything of that nature before this particular Saturday afternoon. If I remember correctly, the ticket window at the movie theater opened about 2:30 p.m., with the movie beginning at 3 p.m. A group of kids would get there 15 to 20 minutes ahead of time and stand in line until the ticket window opened. It was to be the same that day, except for me.

As I was standing in the line that day, with possibly 10 or 15 kids ahead of me, all of a sudden the Spirit of God spoke to my heart and said, "Don't go into this place. Give your heart to Me. You are a chosen vessel to be used exclusively in My service."

I knew it was the Lord, even though many would doubt it. We must understand that the Lord can speak to an 8-year-old the same as He does anyone. At the same time, He can make the individual understand that it is really the Lord who is speaking, even as it was with me that day.

I knew it was the Lord, but yet, I did not make any move to leave the line. About that time, the ticket window opened, and Mrs. Green, who was behind the counter, began to dispense tickets to the young people as they were going inside the theater. There were only three or four other little boys and girls ahead of me when the Lord spoke the second time, saying to me, "You are a chosen vessel to be used in My service. Give your heart to Me and do not go into this place."

About that time, I was standing at the window, and all of a sudden, the spool of tickets jammed. Mrs. Green began trying to untangle it to continue dispensing tickets. I will always believe that the Lord jammed that spool. My quarter was lying on the window ledge, and I reached up and grabbed it. I'll never forget Mrs. Green saying, "Jimmy, do you want to go or not?" I didn't say anything; I just turned and left.

THE FEELING

I walked past the Piggly Wiggly supermarket, Ellis' Five and Dime, and then Doris' Dress Shop. I finally drew abreast of Vogt's Drugstore and walked inside and got an ice cream cone. I walked out and was standing on the curb, eating the ice cream cone, when all of a sudden, the most wonderful feeling I had ever experienced came all over me. It was like 50 pounds rolled away from me. I was a child. I didn't know much of anything about sin, but I knew at that moment that I was born again. I didn't have any doubt about it.

I've often wondered: if I felt that wonderful as an 8-year-old child, how must somebody feel who has been saved from a life of drunkenness, etc.?

As I stood in that line that day in front of the movie house and the Spirit of God spoke to my heart, He was telling me (even though I could not understand it at the time) that I would be greatly involved in world evangelism. He told me that I was a vessel to be used in His service.

As I walked home that day, I was different than when I had left. I was now born again.

As stated, when I arrived home, my mother didn't quite understand why I was home earlier than usual. When she asked me why, I simply said, "I got saved."

I'll never forget the look of perplexity that crossed her countenance.

"What do you mean you got saved?" she asked.

I told her what happened, and she began to weep. I didn't quite understand that because I was so very happy, but looking back, of course, she was weeping because she, too, was happy.

WHY?

Why did the Lord choose that particular time and place to speak to my heart? That I do not know. It would seem that He would have spoken to me when I was in service, but He didn't. Nevertheless, when He spoke and where He spoke made no difference. The facts were that the Lord had spoken, and I knew what He had told me, even though I understood very little about it at the time.

Instantly, I fell in love with the Word of God. I would take to school a Bible that was so small you could fit it inside a small pocket, but yet, having perfect eyesight at that tender age, I could read it. Every day at recess and at noon, I would read the Word of God. The things I didn't understand I would ask my dad about, and if he didn't understand it, he would tell me to go to our pastor. I don't remember if I ever did or not, but I do remember reading the Word of God constantly each and every day. In other words, I fell in love with the Bible from the tender age of 8 forward, and

I believe that's at least one of the reasons the Lord gave me the privilege and the honor of compiling the notes for The Expositor's Study Bible, of which I will have much more to say at a later time.

———◇———

Wonderful story of love,
Tell it to me again,
Wonderful story of love,
Wake the immortal strain.
Angels with rapture announce it,
Shepherds with wonder receive it;
Sinner, oh, won't you believe it?

Wonderful story of love,
Though you are far away,
Wonderful story of love,
Still He does call today,
Calling from Calvary's mountain
Down from the crystal bright fountain,
Even from the dawn of creation.

Wonderful story of love,
Jesus provides a rest,
Wonderful story of love,
For all the pure and blessed;
Rest in those mansions above us,
As with those who've gone on before us,
Singing the rapturous chorus.

AMAZING GRACE

BAPTISM WITH THE HOLY SPIRIT

"Nannie, tell me again how God filled you with the Holy Spirit."

BAPTISM WITH THE HOLY SPIRIT

AS DIFFERENT WAS MY SALVATION, it would prove to be as different with my baptism with the Holy Spirit.

My grandmother was the first one in the Swaggart family to be baptized with the Holy Spirit. As stated, our little church was new, and only a few people in the church were baptized with the Holy Spirit. That was all about to change, but it did not start out that way.

I don't recall anything about the Holy Spirit before the particular time of the story at hand. I'm certain that our pastor, who was a godly brother, preached on the subject, but I have no recollection of it whatsoever. The Holy Spirit used something very strange, just as He did with my salvation.

This must have been only a few weeks since I had given my heart to Christ. As stated, it was the summer months, and I wasn't in school.

I arose that morning, never dreaming this would be a day that would change my life.

I walked into the living room, and my mother and dad were discussing my grandmother—my dad's mother. As stated, my grandmother was the first one in the Swaggart family to be baptized with the Holy Spirit with the evidence of speaking with other tongues, which is the only way one can be baptized. They were discussing my grandmother and were not too happy about the situation. I listened intently as I heard my dad say, "Mama has gone crazy over religion." He then went on to say, "Every time you get around her, she's talking about Jesus. Then she'll start speaking in some kind of language that no one understands. It's gone into fanaticism."

They discussed it for a short period of time, with everything being negative; however, it somehow did not affect me as negative, but rather as positive.

After listening for a little bit and knowing they were unhappy about the situation, still, I wanted to know more.

I hurried outside, got on my bicycle, and rode straight to my grandmother's house. I knocked on the door and in a moment's time, she opened it. I walked into the room and said to her, "Nannie," for that's what I always called her, "my mother and dad were saying something about you being filled with something and speaking funny. What were they talking about?"

She smiled and said, "Jimmy, let me fix a cup of hot tea, and I'll tell you all about it."

She fixed the tea, sat down, and I don't remember that she ever touched it again. She began to tell me what the Lord had done for her. I sat on the floor cross-legged and looked up at her as she related this wonderful incident. She was in a campmeeting that was being conducted very close to Monroe, Louisiana. She had attended that campmeeting with the intention of being baptized with the Holy Spirit, and the Lord did not let her down.

She told me how that the morning service had ended, with most people going a little distance away to find something for lunch. However, she and several other ladies went out under a cope of trees a short distance from the tabernacle to seek the Lord for the infilling of the Holy Spirit.

When a person gets hungry enough to be baptized with the Spirit, nothing else matters. In other words, everything else takes a back seat, so to speak.

FOR THE FIRST TIME...

I sat on the floor and listened to her intently and absorbed every word. Then she got to the place where the Lord filled her with His Spirit, and the moment she started to relate this, the power of God came all over her. At that point, she put up her hands and began to speak with other tongues.

For the first time in my life, I felt the power of God. I looked down at my arms, and chill bumps had broken out all over them. I had never sensed or experienced anything like that. While I had experienced conviction the Saturday afternoon I was saved, as far as the power of God was concerned, this was the first time I had experienced it, at least to my recollection.

I didn't say anything simply because I did not know what to say. That afternoon I was back, asking her to tell me her story all over again, which she always did. Every time she would get to the place where the Lord filled her, she would begin to speak with other tongues, and the power of God would fill that room. Some days I would go as much as three times a day and have her relate the same incident over and over. I grew so hungry myself for the Holy Spirit that I had to hear more about it. Every time that she would relate this experience, she would tell me, "Jimmy, you keep believing, and the Lord is going to give you the very same thing that He has given me."

She filled my heart with faith. Actually, she was one of the greatest persons of faith that I ever knew. She taught me that God is a big God, and she would tell me, "Jimmy, God is a big God, so ask big." I've never forgotten that, and it has helped me to touch this world for Christ. As stated, Nannie was a great woman of faith.

THEN AND NOW

To use a page from the beginning days of my ministry, I go back in my mind's eye to 1955, that is, if I remember the year correctly. The Lord had called me to be an evangelist, so that's what I set out to do. However, to get started seemed to be an impossibility. I knew the Lord had called me, and I knew what I must do, but I did not know how that it could be brought about. The denomination with which we were then associated looked at me (even as they should have), as they did with most every other young preacher getting started, with a sort of wait-and-see attitude. At any rate, those things were actually incidental. It was the Lord who had to make a way for me, or else, no way would be made. He began early teaching me that He was my source and not anything or anyone else.

One particular day, I was greatly perturbed about the situation, and as I was taught to do, I went before the Lord in prayer. At that time, Frances and I lived in a little tiny house trailer—32 feet long and 8 feet wide. Donnie was then about 3 years old. Frances had gone somewhere with him, and during their absence, I went to prayer. I began to importune the Lord, laying these matters before Him, which to me were gigantic, but to Him, of course, were insignificant. At any rate, at a point in time, the Lord brought to my mind a little chorus that we had learned a few weeks earlier. The words were used by the Holy Spirit to minister grandly to my soul and to give me encouragement for what the Lord had called me to do. Those words are:

> *My Lord is able, He is able, I know that He is able, I know my*
> *Lord is able to carry me through.*
> *My Lord is able, He is able, I know that He is able, I know my*
> *Lord is able to carry me through.*
> *For He has healed the broken-hearted, made the blind to see,*
> *healed the sick, raised the dead, and walked upon the sea.*
> *My Lord is able, He is able, I know that He is able, I know my*
> *Lord is able to carry me through.*

The Lord used that little chorus to buttress my soul. I will never forget it. I sat there on the floor, leaning up against the bed at the back of that little trailer as the tears flowed down my face, and the Lord spoke to me saying, "I am able!"

The Lord that day so long ago was telling me that it didn't matter what the problems were, it didn't matter what the difficulties were, and it didn't matter what circumstances said. The Lord said, "I am able."

The other day in prayer, the Lord brought this incident to my thinking once again. I relived those moments for awhile, and then the Lord spoke to my heart and said, "Back in 1955, you were asking Me for meetings wherever the door would open, no matter how small the church was, and now you are asking Me for the entirety of the world."

I sat there on the floor for a few moments, lost in that word the Lord had given me, for that's exactly what was happening. I was importuning the Lord to open doors all over the world for the SonLife Broadcasting Network, which He most definitely was and is doing.

At this time, we are airing the network 24 hours a day, seven days a week in more than 90 million homes in America and nearly 300 million outside of the United States on television, radio, satellite, the Internet, and social media. I am told that, if it is desired, some 2 billion people can now tune in to SBN. In other words, the programming covers a great majority of the entirety of the world, and the Lord held that up to me. He said, "You were asking Me in those days of long ago for just a place to preach, wherever it was, and now you are asking Me for the whole world." He then said, "I was able then, and I am able now. Believe Me for great and mighty things, for I am the God of the impossible. My answer to you now is the same as it was then, I am able."

Let me say that to you as well—whatever your need, whatever it is that you desire, and whatever you must have—*the Lord is able!*

THE PRAYER MEETINGS

I cannot honestly remember if our little church was in revival at that particular time or not, but I do know that the pastor started a prayer meeting each and every morning for whomever would desire to come. It would be conducted at the church. And yes, I was there every morning, asking the Lord to fill me with His Spirit.

Then it happened—while kneeling there at the altar, seeking the Lord for the same experience that my grandmother had, all of a sudden, I felt it come over me. There was a light that seemed to settle down over me, and I have great difficulty trying to explain how it looked. You might say it was liquid light, and yet, there is no such thing, of which I am aware, as liquid light. All of a sudden, just as my grandmother had, I began to speak with other tongues as the Spirit of God gave the utterance.

For several weeks I was hardly able to speak anything in English. Every time that I would open my mouth, I would start speaking in tongues.

My mother sent me to the post office to get a stamp. I remember walking up to the window, placing the nickel on the counter, and proceeded to ask for a stamp, but then I began to speak in tongues. The man behind the counter in the post office looked somewhat perplexed and said to me, "Son, I can't understand what you're saying."

I tried it again and began to speak with other tongues. He looked at me quizzically and said, "What did you say?"

I tried it the third time and began to speak in tongues again. Then, inasmuch as I had embarrassed myself, I grabbed the nickel and ran.

When I got home, strangely enough, I could speak English, but for several weeks, almost all of the time when I opened my mouth, I would begin to speak with tongues. As the old song says:

> *It's real, it's real,*
> *I know, I know it's real;*
> *Thank God the doubts are settled,*
> *I know, I know it's real.*

I have seen and witnessed the moving and operation of the Holy Spirit, which helped me to touch this world for Christ. I have witnessed Him anointing me to preach the gospel which, due to television, resulted in the greatest harvest of souls possibly ever seen. We give the Lord all the praise and all the glory for this.

I personally believe that very little is going to be done for the Lord, if anything, without the mighty baptism with the Holy Spirit. There is no other source for the type of power that we need.

Some may say that some of the great preachers of the past, back in the 1700s, the 1800s, etc., did not have the baptism with the Holy Spirit with the evidence of speaking with other tongues, but yet, saw great things done for the Lord, and that is true. However, they were walking in all the light that they had, and God honored it, really, as He has done with all of us. However, when that light is given, and it is rejected or ignored, the Lord does not take too kindly to that.

Beautifully enough, both my mother and dad were baptized with the Holy Spirit. Actually, it was a short time before the Lord filled me, that is, if I remember the time frame correctly.

They were to learn that this was not fanaticism but, in reality, was the Lord.

There came a sound from heaven,
As of a rushing mighty wind,
It filled every heart with singing,
And it gave them peace within.

The prophet gave this promise,
The Spirit will descend,
And from your innermost being,
A river with no end.

There came a thirsty woman,
That day to Jacob's well,
Her life was ruined and wasted,
Her soul was lost as well.

But she came unto the Master,
And He forgave her all her sin,
And said, If you drink of the water I give you,
You'll never thirst again.

There is a river that flows from deep within,
There is a fountain that frees the soul from sin,
Come to these waters, there is a vast supply,
There is a river that never shall run dry.

AMAZING GRACE

CHAPTER 4

THE PIANO

"If you give me
this talent,
I will never use it
in the world."

THE PIANO

THERE'S NOTHING IN THE world like childlike faith. It simply believes, and it is done.

Before I was baptized with the Holy Spirit, I had it in my childish mind that the Lord would not answer any prayer of mine until I was first filled with the Spirit. Of course, I was wrong, but not by very much.

I remember very vividly refusing to ask the Lord for anything until He filled me with His Spirit. Where I got this, I don't know. Why this came into my mind, once again, I simply don't know. I don't recall that I ever heard anyone say anything of this nature, but that's what I believed at the time. However, when the Lord baptized me with the Holy Spirit, that blew the hinges off the door, so to speak. I believed that I could ask the Lord for anything, and He would do it. Of course, I was only 8 years of age, but I had an amazing faith at that time.

I am positive that the faith that I had was strengthened on a daily basis by my grandmother. She was one of the greatest women of faith I ever knew. She would tell me in those early years, "Jimmy, you will see a harvest of souls such as the world has never seen before." She would continue, "I will not see it. I will go on to be with the Lord, but you will see it." I can see her now in my mind's eye with an enraptured look on her face as she seemed to see into the spirit world. Marvelously so, she was right.

In my childish mind, I decided that I was going to ask the Lord to give me the talent to play the piano. I don't know why that I chose that instrument.

Many might say that music ran in our family, so it had nothing to do with the Lord. It is definitely correct that music runs in our family. Both my mother and dad played instruments. My cousin, Jerry Lee Lewis, was one of the top rock 'n' roll stars of the 1960s and later, with him at times even beating out Elvis Presley. Then, there is my cousin, Mickey Gilley, who had 17 number one country and western hits. Also, there were three other cousins who played piano. Yes, music runs in our family; however, I have other relatives who cannot play any musical instruments.

Of course, at 8 years of age, the fact that music ran in our family never entered my mind. I was going to ask the Lord to give me the talent to play the piano, and I believed that He would hear my petition.

We were in revival. The evangelist would later (many years later) become the district superintendent of the Louisiana district of the Assemblies of God. He played piano and played it well. I will never forget the night in question.

LOOK WHAT THE LORD HAS DONE

All of the time the dear brother was preaching that night (I was sitting beside my dad), I was importuning the Lord to give me the talent to play the piano. I don't know why I chose that time, and I don't know why I chose that place or moment, but I did.

In my petition I promised the Lord that if He would give me the talent, I would never use it in the ways of the world. Being 8 years of age, I did not know too much about the world, but I had heard about night clubs. So, I told the Lord, "I'll never use the talent in a night club if You will help me to play."

I could hardly wait for the service to end. When it did, I slowly walked onto the platform, where stood an old upright piano. I looked down at the white and black keys and placed my fingers on those keys and began to make chords. I did not know what the chords were, but I was making them nonetheless.

When we got home that night after service, my dad asked me, "Jimmy, where did you learn those chords I heard you playing on the piano after service?"

He then continued, "Have you been up at Aunt Stella's?" for she had a piano.

I said, "No, sir."

He said, "Has Sister Culbreth taught you those chords?" She was our pastor's wife and played the piano fairly well.

Again I said, "No, sir."

"Well, where did you learn those chords you were playing tonight after service?" he asked.

My answer was very truthful and straight to the point. I said, "I asked the Lord tonight to give me the talent to play the piano, and I suppose He has already started."

That was my answer—to the point and simple, but yet ever so truthful.

No, I did not learn to play immediately, but little by little, the Lord began to help me, and in a short period of time, I learned to play fairly well.

Along with the talent that He gave me for that particular instrument, He also gave me an understanding of what the Holy Spirit wants as it regards music, and I speak of praise and worship.

Our music, for which I give the Lord all the praise and all the glory, has spread around the world. In fact, at the time of this writing, I have sold some 17 million recordings. Once again, we give the Lord all the praise and all the glory for that. The Lord has helped me to touch millions with my music, and I do not exaggerate. Once again, look what the Lord has done. Also, I can quickly say that I have kept my promise to Him as it regards staying true to my calling. I have never used my talent in the world, but always for the glory of God.

Many times I've had people ask me, "Have you ever been tempted to go into the world with your music?"

I can honestly say before God that temptation has never affected me one bit whatsoever—not even in the days when my cousins were making mountains of money, and Frances and I were just beginning in evangelistic work, with money nonexistent. There was never one single time that I had a thought of going in any other direction.

I remember recording in Nashville one time. If I remember correctly, it was at Columbia Studios. We had a five or 10-minute break between songs, and I had walked down the hall to get some water or something. I passed a man, and he stopped me and said, "You're Jimmy Swaggart."

I nodded in the affirmative.

He said to me, "I see your records everywhere I go. Who is your distributor?"

In the record business, distribution is the name of the game. When he asked me that question, I softly said, "The Holy Spirit."

I'll never forget his answer. As I turned and walked away, I heard him say, "The Holy *who*?"

However, I wasn't joking. It has been the Holy Spirit all the time who has helped us to do what we've done with our music.

At the same time, I will have to give much of the credit to Frances. Even though she is not a musician whatsoever, she saw something in my music that even I didn't see. Through her encouragement, and I mean strong encouragement, we placed an emphasis on the music that, looking back, I now know was exactly what the Lord wanted done.

There is no power in the world like music, other than the preaching of the gospel. In fact, music and singing that's anointed by the Holy Spirit is the most powerful form of praise and worship that there is.

How do I know that?

The Holy Spirit delegated the longest book in the Bible to be music and singing, and, of course, I speak of the book of Psalms. All 150 of the psalms are actually songs that were originally written by the Holy Spirit and given to David and others. Other than the preaching of the gospel, nothing can touch the heart of individuals as anointed music and singing can.

If you will notice, I included the musical instrumentation. The Lord anoints me to play the piano exactly as He anoints me to sing, and once again, I give Him all the praise and all the glory.

LET ME GIVE YOU AN EXAMPLE

My cousin, Jerry Lee Lewis, was brought up in the same church that I was, and he was saved and baptized with the Holy Spirit as a young boy. When he was making millions of dollars and selling millions of records, something happened that would test my faith.

If I remember correctly, the year was 1958. While Frances and I had begun evangelistic work in 1955, we launched out full-time in 1958. However, I must quickly add that launching out created no headlines anywhere. At any rate, I was preaching a meeting at our home church in Ferriday, Louisiana. It was Sunday and, after the service, there was a dinner on the grounds which was somewhat common in those days. A table was set up at the back of the church, and the ladies of the church, what few there were, brought the food.

Frances and I were standing, eating, and enjoying the fellowship, when all of a sudden, there turns off the main highway, onto the side road that led to the church, a brand-new Cadillac.

Of course, everyone's eyes were glued to this tremendous automobile, which was then the finest in the world. It drove up very close to where I was standing and stopped.

My Uncle Elmo, Jerry Lee's dad, quickly got out of the car and, of course, everyone was glad to see him. Uncle Elmo was a gregarious individual, with such a personality that everyone who met him liked him. That's the kind of person he was. I suspect that Jerry Lee got a lot of his singing talent from his dad because the man could sing. Be that as it may, as the people gathered around that beautiful car and were admiring it, my uncle walked over to me.

He said, "Jimmy, I have the greatest news."

I wondered what he was about to say.

He said, "I've just left Sun Records in Memphis, Tennessee, and I've come to get you. You are going to join the Sun label. They're starting a gospel line, and you are to be the first artist. Sam Phillips has sent for you. I'm to have you in Memphis in the morning."

At that time, Sun Records was at least one of the most powerful recording labels in the world, having started Elvis Presley, my cousin Jerry Lee Lewis, Carl Perkins, Johnny Cash, and a host of others. To be sure, this was good news, and I opened my mouth to say "I'm ready," when the Holy Spirit checked me.

I must have looked a little strange, because my uncle said to me, "Jimmy, did you hear what I just said?"

I looked at him for a moment and said, "Yes, I heard you, and I am very, very grateful. But I can't do it."

Uncle Elmo said, "Son, I know you need the money. Your car is falling all to pieces. Every time I see you, you're wearing the same suit. As well, every time I see Frances, she has on the same dress." He then said, "A week from now, you could be driving a Cadillac exactly like the one I've got here."

A tremendous battle was raging in my mind. To be sure, this offer was very, very enticing. Besides that, how could it hurt, considering that it was gospel music? I didn't really know what to say to my uncle, except what I had already stated. I didn't understand it myself. Why could I not go, considering, as stated, that it was gospel music? I responded to him that he should thank Sam Phillips very profusely for the offer that was made. I tried to tell my uncle how much I appreciated it, because I didn't want to seem ungrateful.

Uncle Elmo, who really wasn't living for God, looked at me and said, "Jimmy, I think I understand." He hugged my neck, and I thanked him profusely and asked him again to thank Sam Phillips for the invitation. Then he got in that Cadillac and drove away.

I wish I had the vocabulary to properly express exactly how I felt at that moment. My uncle was right. Our car was falling to pieces, and we really did not know where the next dollar was coming from. I overheard one of the dear ladies nearby say, "Did you hear what he just did? He turned down that offer."

I walked away, actually going into the little church. There was a broom and mop closet there, and I stepped inside of it, to get alone with the Lord. For a few moments I poured out my heart to God, asking Him why I could not do this. It was gospel music, and, on the surface, it seemed like an answer to prayer, especially considering how much Frances and I needed the money. Yet the Holy Spirit had said no.

After a few minutes I sensed the presence of the Lord, and He spoke to me in answer to my questions. He did so with just two words. He said, "Trust Me." That was all, just the two words. No explanation was given, no reasons why, just two words: trust Me.

When I was an 8-year-old child, the Lord had given me this talent, and He had the right to order whatever was to be done. I stood there that day by myself and said, "Lord, I will do exactly what You want."

We must understand that, at times, the Lord will tell us to do things or not do certain things, which of themselves are not wrong; but the reason is, those things are not, whatever they might be, His will. The Lord wants to lead us; He wants to guide us, and we had better be careful that the offers which come from the world do not have strings attached, and they almost always do.

So what did the Lord mean when He said, "Trust Me"?

He did not explain it further then, but I was to learn through the years exactly what He meant. He meant that He had given me the talent, and He would do the promoting, would do the anointing, and would do the distribution, and He did not need help from anyone else. And that is exactly what has happened.

I've never signed with a company, even the Christian labels. I've always trusted the Lord, and He has helped us to sell, as stated, multiple millions of recordings down through the years. Above all, these recordings have been anointed by the Holy Spirit, which means that they have been a blessing to those who needed that blessing.

Once again, what a mighty God we serve.

———✕———

Look away from the Cross to the glittering crown,
From your cares, weary ones, look away!
There's a home for the soul where no sorrows can come,
And where pleasures will never decay.

Though the burdens of life may be heavy to bear,
And your crosses and trials severe
There's a beautiful hand that is beckoning, "Come,"
And no heartaches and sighings are there.

'Mid the conflicts, the battles, the struggles and strife
Bravely onward your journey pursue,
Look away from the Cross to that glittering crown,
That's awaiting in heaven for you.

AMAZING GRACE

CHAPTER 5

GIFTS OF THE SPIRIT

"These are gifts of the Spirit and not gifts of man. He alone can bestow these gifts as He alone can empower these gifts."

GIFTS OF THE SPIRIT

I BELIEVE THE HOLY SPIRIT desires that every believer have at least one of the nine gifts of the Holy Spirit—word of wisdom, word of knowledge, faith, gifts of healing, working of miracles, prophecy, discerning of spirits, divers kinds of tongues, and interpretation of tongues. One reason these gifts are no more prominent than they are is simply because so little is taught about them. When I was a boy, not only did I learn about these wonderful gifts in church, but shortly after I was baptized in the Holy Spirit, I experienced them.

About that time, we were having prayer meetings at the church every morning. Then, sometimes, actually, most of the time, we would go to my aunt's home in the afternoon and have prayer meeting again.

It was then that the Lord spoke through others and me. At that time, He told me about the ministry that I would have—that it would be in the field of evangelism. There were times when I would go into a trance, and when I would come out of the trance,

I would think that only 15 or 20 minutes had passed when, in reality, several hours had passed.

One particular morning, the Lord spoke through me and said, "A bomb is being constructed that is so powerful that just one of these weapons will destroy a major city." This was in 1943.

At that time, the atomic bomb was being developed; however, there was such secrecy surrounding that thing that it was known only by a few people in the nation. While the word *atomic* was not used in that which the Lord gave me, still, the description was that of an atomic bomb.

These messages went on for several weeks and, of course, were proven correct when the two cities of Nagasaki, Japan, and Hiroshima, Japan, were totally destroyed by one bomb each.

WHY?

Why would the Lord give such a word to an 8-year-old child?

That I cannot answer. However, this I do know: The Lord never makes a mistake and always has a reason for what He does. And yet, the Scripture says, *"Out of the mouth of babes"* (Ps. 8:2).

The gifts of the Spirit are not limited to any class of people, be it age, nationality, or gender. The Lord uses whom He wills and in the way that He desires. Some may endeavor to deny the Lord using an 8-year-old child in this manner, but they cannot deny the veracity of what was proclaimed. As stated, even though the word *atomic* was never used, still, the description was exact.

When it comes to the gifts of the Spirit, people often get confused between a word of wisdom and word of knowledge.

A word of wisdom has to do with people, places, or things pertaining to the future, whereas a word of knowledge has to do with people, places, and things pertaining to the present or the past (I Cor. 12:8-10). Very often these two gifts operate together.

WORD OF KNOWLEDGE

I could give several illustrations as to how the word of knowledge has worked through this evangelist, but I think the following will suffice—an experience that happened 40 years after the word about the atomic bomb.

PREACHERS PUT IN JAIL

If I remember correctly, it was 1983. Several Baptist preachers had been put in jail in the state of Nebraska because they would not comply with the demands of the state regarding their private Christian school. The news was in all the papers. Everyone was wondering how such a thing could be—preachers put in jail because of some rules, which they felt, in all good conscience, they could not comply with.

Somebody in Washington sent for three preachers to come to that city, hoping that a means could be devised so that the preachers in Nebraska could be released from jail. I was one of those preachers.

If my memory serves me correctly, we met in one of the large rooms in the Old Executive Office Building that is very near the White House.

THE PRESIDENT'S CABINET

The room was filled with lawyers. In fact, there were so many lawyers there that many of them had to stand against the wall. Almost all of the president's cabinet was present, and I speak of President Reagan. Ed Meese, attorney general of the United States, was there. In fact, he was seated right next to me on my right. As well, the Secretary of State, James Baker, and the national security advisor, Robert McFarland, were also present.

Members of the president's cabinet spoke, stating that they would do anything that was legal to get these men released from jail, as long as it would not embarrass the president. Constitutional lawyers tried to figure out something from a legal viewpoint.

The other two preachers spoke, and I honestly don't remember what they said.

Attorney General Meese, who was seated right next to me, began to speak, and, while he was speaking, the Holy Spirit began to deal with my heart, giving me a word of knowledge as it regarded the situation. I'll be frank with you, I thought, "Lord, if this isn't You, then I'll look like a fool."

The Lord gently spoke to my heart, telling me that as soon as the attorney general finished speaking, I should speak up and give to this group of men what the Lord had told me.

GO AHEAD

I waited for the attorney general to finish. No, I did not mention to these men that it was the Lord who gave me this, and for all the obvious reasons. When the attorney general finished, there was a brief silence, and the Lord said, "Go ahead."

I cleared my throat and began to speak, and, of course, all eyes were on me. To say that I was nervous would be an understatement. I asked those present, and I speak of the president's cabinet, "Isn't the president going to address the nation tonight?"

One of the cabinet members spoke up and said, "Yes, he is."

I said, "Why not have the president mention this situation in Nebraska? That will draw a lot of attention to that which is happening and might cause the officials there to think twice and release these men."

When I finished speaking, a silence gripped the entire room. All of a sudden, the leading constitutional lawyer in the room, who was seated at the head of the table, jumped to his feet and slammed his fist down on the table and said, "Why didn't I think of that?"

The national security advisor to the president spoke up and said, "I'm writing the president's speech. I will make mention of this thing, and I know exactly what to say."

That night, President Reagan addressed the nation, mentioned the situation at hand, and the next morning, the preachers were released from jail. That was a word of knowledge that the Holy Spirit revealed to me. No, the Lord does not reveal such to me every time. In fact, He has only done such a few times in all of my life and living. This tells us that we as believers do not order the Holy Spirit around, but we rather wait on Him that He may give us in due time that which He wishes us to have.

HEALING

Throughout the New Testament, illness and disease are associated with the forces hostile to God and to humanity. Throughout the Gospels, Jesus is always healing, never once causing illness. While the weaknesses of humanity reflect the reality of human alienation from God, Jesus' attitude and actions show that God is and yearns to be man's healer. To see illness only as punishment is to misread the nature of God and to misunderstand the nature of those forces that distort human experience.

A PERSONAL HEALING

I can't remember exactly, but I think I was about 10 years old. For the previous six months or more during that time, I had come to the place that I was constantly nauseated. At times, I would pass out, meaning that I would literally go unconscious. In fact, this happened several times while I was at school. The last time it happened, the principal called my parents, and they were told, "If something is not done, Jimmy is going to have to be taken out of school." Then the principal added, "We don't want him dying on our hands."

In fact, my mother and dad had taken me to several doctors, with all the ensuing examinations, and it was all to no avail. In other words, they simply did not know what was wrong with me. They ruled out malaria, plus several other things, and whatever it was they tried seemingly did not work. Instead of getting better, I was getting worse.

I fully believe that Satan was trying to kill me. He knew how the Lord would use me in the future, so that was his way of stopping it. Thank the Lord, he didn't succeed.

During all of this, I was prayed for several times. We had a godly pastor at our little church. He was young, but he loved the Lord and fully believed that the Lord healed the sick. Besides that, my parents, my grandmother, and my aunt strongly believed in the power of God and the ability of the Lord to heal the sick and to perform miracles, irrespective of the problem. Nevertheless, despite their anointing me with oil any number of times and repeatedly praying for me, I did not grow better, but rather worse.

THE MANNER IN WHICH THE LORD DOES THINGS

Actually, there is no person who fully understands why the Lord does things in the manner in which they are carried out. We know that He is omnipotent, meaning all-powerful, and omniscient, meaning all-knowing, and omnipresent, meaning that He is everywhere. Consequently, He has means about which we know nothing.

On this particular day in question, actually a Sunday, my parents had invited the pastor and his wife to go with us to lunch after the service, which they did. I remember that when my parents invited Brother Culbreth, our pastor, he stated that first of all, they had to go to a particular brother's house and pray for him. It was a family that all of us knew, and they attended our little church.

That Sunday, and it must have been about 12:30 or 1 p.m., we went to the little three-room, shotgun house to pray for the brother in question.

I remember the pastor and his wife, my mother and dad, along with my baby sister and me, walking to the back room where the brother was. He was anointed with oil and prayer was offered for him regarding whatever type of illness he had.

We then all walked back to the front room and were standing there, in effect, making small talk with the lady of the house, planning to leave in a moment.

THE BALL OF FIRE

My dad spoke up and said to the pastor, "Brother Culbreth, please pray for Jimmy. If the Lord doesn't do something for him, we're going to have to take him out of school."

Brother Culbreth was standing there with a bottle of oil in his hand, with which he had just anointed the dear brother in question. I remember him smiling and walking across the floor to where I was standing. I can still see that room. My dad, the pastor, and his wife were standing against the back wall. My mother was to my right, along with the wife of the dear brother for whom we had just prayed. I was standing next to the door that led outside.

Brother Culbreth walked over to where I was standing, took the top off the little bottle of oil, placed a little of it on his finger, and anointed my head, with all of us beginning to pray. In fact, he had done that any number of times. But this time something happened, and it happened instantly.

It was like a ball of fire, something about the size of a softball, which started at the top of my head and slowly went down the back of my body, all the way to my feet, yet without any pain. Even though I was only 10 years old, and, as stated, I had been prayed for any number of times previous to this, I knew that now I was healed. There was no doubt about it; I knew I was healed.

I don't remember a great moving of the Spirit that took place in the room at that moment. I do remember everyone there praising the Lord, but again, we always did that. However, I knew I was healed.

The sickness left immediately, never came back, and I have enjoyed excellent health from then until now. I did have a stint put in an artery of my heart in February 2001, and I've had the normal colds, and one time, I even had what is referred to as walking pneumonia. However, relatively speaking, I've enjoyed excellent health. I've traveled all over the world and eaten food that should have made anyone sick but without any adverse effect to my physical body. I give the Lord all the praise and glory.

GREAT TRUTHS

First of all, I'm so glad that my parents attended a church where the pastor believed in healing. It was very small, and as far as most people were concerned, it was of little significance. However, this pastor and most of the few people who attended this little assembly were godly, and that's all that mattered. Had my parents attended a church that didn't believe in divine healing, I don't really believe I would be alive today.

Second, I'm glad my parents didn't quit praying for me after not seeing any success the first time, or even after several times. Had they stopped, again, I don't believe I would be alive today.

———⊷✕⊶———

I care not today what the morrow may bring
If shadow or sunshine or rain,
The Lord I know rules over everything,
And all of my worry is vain.

Tho' tempests may blow and the storm clouds rise,
Obscuring the brightness of life,
I'm never alarmed at the overcast skies,
The Master looks on at the strife.

I know that He safely will carry me through,
No matter what evils betide,
Why should I then care, though the tempests may blow,
If Jesus waits close by my side.

Our Lord will return to this earth some sweet day
Our troubles will then all be o'er
The Master so gently will lead us away,
Beyond that blessed heavenly shore.

AMAZING
GRACE

DREAMS AND VISIONS

"You will not do it;
I will stop you."

DREAMS AND VISIONS

THE FIRST DREAM RECORDED in the Bible concerned Abraham. Abimelech, the king of Gerar, was planning to take Sarah for his wife. Sarah was Abraham's wife, but Abraham had not been truthful with Abimelech. At any rate, the Bible says, *"But God came to Abimelech in a dream by night, and said to him, Behold, you are but a dead man, for the woman which you have taken; for she is a man's wife"* (Gen. 20:3).

Then we have the dreams of Joseph (Gen. 37:5-9). Afterward, we have the dream of Pharaoh, which was one of the most important in history. It was a dream, incidentally, that was interpreted by Joseph regarding what it meant (Gen. 41:8, 32). Then, there are the dreams that Joseph, the husband of Mary, had concerning the boy Jesus (Mat. 1:20, 2:22).

Of course, these are only a few of the many that the Bible illustrates, but I think it suffices to say that the Lord does at times speak to people in dreams.

And yet, there are dreams, and then there are dreams. Just because a person is a believer, it doesn't necessarily mean that every dream he has is from the Lord. Some are, but some aren't.

Over the course of my life, the Lord has given me several dreams and visions, and He continues to do so. These that I'm about to share with you have deeply impacted my life and ministry.

WORLD EVANGELISM

I was about 10 years old when the Lord gave me the dream that I will relate to you. Of course, at that age I really did not understand the dream, but I most definitely have come to understand it in later times. Let me lay a little foundation before I relate that which the Lord gave me.

During those times, from 8 years old until about 11 years old, I was in a prayer meeting somewhere almost every day of my life. Actually, in a cope of woods near our house, I had found a log where a tree had fallen, and I made an altar out of it. I would go out there several times a day and kneel beside that log and seek the face of the Lord. As stated, this was almost on a daily basis, especially in the months when I was not in school.

In a number of these prayer meetings, I felt that the Lord spoke to me and told me that I would be an evangelist. As well, he related to me that I would be involved in world evangelism, even though I really did not understand at that time what it all meant. I just knew that I would preach in countries all over the world, which, of course, has come to pass exactly as the Lord said.

As I've already stated, my grandmother encouraged me greatly during this time. She encouraged me to believe in God in that He could do great and mighty things. She instilled that into my mind, into my heart, into my thinking, and into my very being. Consequently, for everything that we've ever seen done for the Lord, I would have to give my grandmother much of the credit. She was a woman of great faith, and she taught me the same thing. As I have related elsewhere in this volume, her great word to me more than once was, "Jimmy, God is a big God, so ask big."

Through her I learned to believe the Lord, to expect great things from Him, and to believe that He answered prayer and could do anything.

THE NIGHT IN QUESTION

Because of what this dream meant, I think it was and is extremely important.

I dreamed I was standing in front of our house in Ferriday, Louisiana. I looked to my right and suspended in air was a globe of this planet, which was about the size of a basketball. If I remember the dream correctly, I could see the continents as the ball slowly turned. Even though I was only 10 years old, I knew it was a portrayal of this planet called Earth.

Then, all of a sudden, there was a figure like a man standing very close to it. He just suddenly appeared, and somehow I knew this was Satan. Amazingly, I registered no fear whatsoever. I just stared at him.

For a period of time, he looked at this ball that was slowly turning, symbolizing this planet, and said nothing. Finally, he turned to me and said, "You will not do it; I will stop you."

I said nothing but just absorbed what was said. He then turned back and looked at this ball again. Once again, it was for a period of time, without him making any remarks. He then turned to me one more time and said the same words exactly as before: "You will not do it; I will stop you."

I did not really understand at the time what he was talking about. It really did not make any sense to me. What was he meaning, "You will not do it"? And what did he mean, "I will stop you"?

Of course, in the years that followed, I came to understand what was being said that particular night when I had that dream.

I firmly believe the following that I am about to relate, and I believe that the Lord told me this in later years.

This was in about 2005. In prayer one morning, long before daylight, there was a powerful moving of the Holy Spirit over my heart and life. Then, the Lord spoke to my heart and said, "Your situation is very much akin to that of Job."

Now, please don't misunderstand. I do not even remotely consider myself to have been able to stand in the shadow of one such as Job, but yet, I know beyond the shadow of a doubt that the Lord spoke that word to me.

JOB

That particular morning in 2005, as I drove to the office before daylight, which was my usual custom, I switched on SonLife Radio, and a track was playing of the great song, "Job's God is True." I had recorded it a few months earlier, and for some reason, they were playing the track over radio. At any rate, the Spirit of God filled the car. I have learned that anytime the presence of the Lord is prevalent, the Lord is saying something. We may not learn then exactly what He is saying, but He is most definitely saying something.

When I arrived at the office, I went to prayer as was my usual custom. In my seeking His face that morning, the Lord took me back to the year 1954. Frances was pregnant at that time with Donnie. At any rate, we journeyed from our home in northeast Louisiana to Baton Rouge where Brother David Nunn was conducting a giant tent crusade in the city. If I remember correctly, we were there on the first night. Brother Nunn began to sing a song, which, at that time, I had never heard. It was "Job's God is True." As he was singing, all of a sudden, something came over me in such a way that I had never experienced before. It was the presence of God, but it was in a different way than I had ever known.

I began to weep and then to sob, and it became so intense that for a short period of time, I thought I wouldn't be able to stand it. When I was able to finally gather my composure and look around, I could not see anyone else who was affected. I knew the Lord had moved upon me, but I did not really understand the reason. As stated, it was a moving of the Spirit such as I had never experienced in my life.

I CAME TO UNDERSTAND WHAT HE WAS DOING

That night, as Brother Nunn sang that song about Job, the Lord was telling me that I was going to have to go through a trial that in some sense of the word would be similar to that of Job. He made that very real to me that morning in 2005 as I began to understand that which had taken place way back in 1954.

Then, the Lord spoke to me again and said, "But remember, I gave Job twice as much as I had allowed to be taken from him."

The Lord was showing me that night way back in 1954 that He would use me in world evangelism. I firmly believe that Satan said to the Lord that if the Lord was going to give me certain attributes to help me carry out the task of world evangelism, then Satan was to have certain latitude to stop me. I believe that as the Lord gave Satan certain latitude with Job, He did with me as well. In a sense, I am saying that I believe the Lord spoke that to my heart that early morning hour in 2005. However, anything that the Lord does in such a fashion, He always gives the individual enough power and strength to come out victoriously.

WORLD EVANGELISM

As I dictate these notes, our television programming is going out 24 hours a day, seven days a week, over a great part of this world. Darryl Rains, who heads up our computer department at the ministry, said to me the other day that if so desired, some 2 billion people are able to pick up SonLife Broadcasting Network at this time. And yet, we continue to add cities and countries even up to this present time. In fact, just two days ago, I signed the contracts to start airing our programming 24 hours a day, seven days a week, in São Paulo,

Brazil, and Rio de Janeiro, Brazil. These are two of the largest cities in the world. Actually, it is believed that São Paulo has a population of some 50 million.

THE COMMISSION

A dream is when you are asleep, and a vision is when you are awake.

It was 1985. That morning, as I did every morning, I drove my car close to the railroad tracks that are about a mile from our home. My custom was to sit in the car and read the Word of God for a period of time and then walk down the tracks, seeking the face of the Lord. I did that on this particular morning also. There were almost no houses or places of business there whatsoever at that time, whereas now, the area is filled with such. At any rate, that morning as I began to seek the face of the Lord, there was no warning regarding what the Lord was about to show me.

All of a sudden as I was walking down that track, the scene changed in front of me in all points. The entire earth, it seemed, was planted with cotton. The stalks were filled, with the bolls full, so much so that there was not a green leaf on any stalk. I was raised in northeast Louisiana where cotton is one of the staple crops, so I know a little bit about it. As I looked at this harvest, I had never seen such cotton in all of my life. Then I looked to my left, which was out of the east according to the way I was walking, and I saw a storm that was coming. The clouds were inky black, so black, in fact, that they were such as I had never seen before as it regarded weather. It was coming down on this cotton that stretched over the horizon in every direction.

I then looked quite a distance from me ahead, and I saw two (if I remember correctly) mechanical pickers that were gathering the harvest. Then, for the first time, the Lord spoke to me.

HE SAID...

"I have called certain ministries for particular localities around the world, but I have called this ministry alone for the entirety of the world." He then said, "Don't fail Me because there is no one else to carry out this task."

He then added, "I am going to hold back the storm for a period of time until the harvest can be gathered."

The events that followed made it almost impossible for me to carry out this task. Frances, Donnie, Gabriel, and a host of friends did all that they could do, but it seemed that the task was impossible. Jim Woolsey was the one who kept trying when I, in my own heart, felt that it was useless. I was to find out that God would honor his faith in such a way as to seem impossible, but it did happen.

Jim took some 30 trips to Moscow in what was then the Soviet Union in order to get the telecast on the air. I thought that Jim was wasting his time. I have to be frank with you, it was not my faith that did this, but rather his.

At long last the day came. I think it was in 1989 that the officials in charge of communications in the Soviet Union gave us TV-1 in order for us to air our one-hour program every Sunday morning. TV-1 covered some 7,000 repeater stations and reached the entirety of what was then the Soviet Union.

For the approximate three years that we were on the air there every week, we received over a million letters, and I'm not exaggerating, from people who had given their hearts and lives to Christ. In fact, it's quite possible that there would not be a Russia today had it not been for the telecast.

I'll explain: when the communists tried to take the country back again, President Yeltsin gave instructions for the telecast to be played over and over again in order to, hopefully, calm the people, which it did.

At any rate, about three years ago (2015), I was praying about our programming, which was going into country after country, when the Lord began to move upon my heart.

He spoke to me and said, "The commission I gave to you in 1985 is still in force." He then added, "Get it done."

I can't tell you how I felt. For a short period of time, I could not say anything. I had thought that we had failed at that effort, and there was no more that could be done, but here the Lord was telling me, "It is still in force. Get it done."

That's the reason we go on television anywhere in the world that the Lord opens the door. To be sure, the Evil One has tried his best to stop us exactly as he said to me in that dream in 1945, but he has not been successful. By the grace of God, he will not be successful.

World evangelism is my calling. That's what the Lord was saying to me that day in 1943 when I stood in front of that moving picture theatre, and He said, "Don't go into this place. Give your heart to Me, for you are a chosen vessel to be used exclusively in My service." He was speaking then of world evangelism, even though I did not understand it at the time.

The words of the apostle Paul come down to us, "*How shall they hear without a preacher?*" (Rom. 10:14).

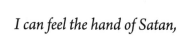

I can feel the hand of Satan,
As the tempter pressed me sore;
He has been before the Father,
Asking leave to tempt me more.

I can hear the Father grant it
Saying do not touch his life;
Though you crush him he'll not falter,
He will rise above the strife.

Though I struggle, I'll not stagger,
By His grace, I'll make it through;
For His grace is all sufficient,
And I know that God is true.

When I have looked all around me,
And His face I cannot see;
Then I know that through the lattice,
He beholdeth even me.

Though God slay me, I will trust Him,
I shall then come forth as gold,
For I know that He still liveth,
For I feel Him in my soul.

AMAZING GRACE

CHAPTER 7

FRANCES

"The part that Frances plays
in this ministry is beyond my
ability to portray. It's been her
wisdom, faith, and consecration
that helped us survive what
seemed to be impossible."

FRANCES

IT WAS SOMEWHERE AROUND 1950 when my dad decided to build a church in the little town of Wisner, Louisiana. And when I say little, I mean they had the monstrous population of approximately 300, but I will ever be grateful to Wisner for just one.

Sometime after dad got the church up and going, my sister Jeanette informed me that there was a new girl who had just joined the choir, and I should meet her.

I still remember the first time I saw her. She was standing in the choir, third from the end. I asked my sister what her name was and Jeanette said, "Frances Anderson." The prettiest name for the prettiest girl I'd ever seen. That was it for me, she was the one.

Other than my salvation, the greatest thing that ever happened to me—and in every way—was Frances. It truly was the Lord who made this match, for which I will ever be grateful.

I personally believe that Frances is presently one of the most influential women in the world as it regards the gospel of

Jesus Christ. Her daily television program, which is two hours each day, goes out to almost the entirety of the world. In fact, of all the programs on our network, hers is the most popular.

She has an amazing ability to read people, which is far greater than mine. In fact, as far as personnel is concerned, she attends to that at the ministry, which numbers more than 300 people.

EVANGELISTIC WORK

When we went into full-time evangelistic work, she was my greatest booster. Strangely enough, she had been raised in a Methodist church, but when the Lord saved her and baptized her with the Holy Spirit, she became one of the most ardent Pentecostals that you would ever meet. Along with all of that, she taught Donnie through the Calvert School by correspondence for several years, and in all of that time, she never missed one single service in church. I'm speaking of church every night.

When Donnie entered junior high school, he began attending particular schools. Actually, he attended 32 schools before his high school graduation in Baton Rouge. He thought that changing schools every four weeks was normal. Of course, it wasn't, but it did teach him many things as it regarded making the best out of something that was not so good.

THUS SAITH THE LORD

I remember a meeting we were conducting in a small church in Alabama. Small as it was, still, the Lord was blessing tremendously, with many souls being saved and the crowds overflowing the place. But yet, we had been on the field for many years, and Frances and I were exhausted. We had no home except for an automobile, or, in some of the places, a third-rate motel.

A church in Baton Rouge was in need of a pastor, and to be frank, I wanted to take their offer to be the pastor. We had traveled for years, and, as stated, both of us were very, very tired.

One Saturday morning, after hearing of this church and being asked to take it, I went over to the church where we were conducting the meeting to seek the Lord about the matter. During the course of my petition to Him, He spoke to my heart and said that He had called me to be an evangelist, and that call was not lifted. I had told the Lord that I wanted His perfect will, with no desire whatsoever for a permissive will—only His perfect will.

When the Lord spoke that to my heart, I immediately forgot the church in Baton Rouge, at least as far as being its pastor.

At that time, I had no knowledge whatsoever of what the future would hold. I did not know or have the faintest idea that in a short time, the Lord would put us on daily radio all over the nation. I didn't know that television would come shortly thereafter and reach a great part of the world. I didn't realize that great citywide meetings would be that which the Lord would lead. Of course, the Lord knew all of this. I firmly believe that had I demanded my own way in that situation, these things that I have just mentioned, which have touched the world, quite possibly would never have happened.

In all of this, not one single time did Frances ever complain. She was called of God just the same as I was called of God. I believe that with all of my heart.

THE FIRST ALBUM

My first record, *Some Golden Daybreak,* which I felt was poorly done, was selling fairly well at our meetings, but Jerry Lee kept after me to record an album at Sun Records.

"Let's do it right this time," he said. "I'll get the musicians for you, and I think I can even get Sam Phillips to give you the studio time. The whole thing won't cost you a dime."

At that price, I could hardly refuse his offer. "Okay," I agreed.

But when we got to Memphis, we found out it wouldn't be that easy. We learned that Sun was a union studio, and since I wasn't a member of the musician's union, I couldn't record there. I offered to join, but the process would take a while. They couldn't get me in before our scheduled studio time to record.

At his home in Memphis, Jerry Lee and I searched for a solution. We called the musician's union and explained the situation, but they had their rules. We reached out to other studios to try and record elsewhere, but to no avail.

About that time, one of Jerry Lee's house guests (he always had a group that followed him on tours and to the studios) asked, "What are y'all doing?"

Jerry Lee said, "We're trying to get a record cut for my cousin, but we can't get the studio because the union has threatened to shut us down."

This man, who wore a permanent five o'clock shadow and sunglasses said, "They what?"

Jerry Lee rephrased our problem. "We've got to cut this record today because my cousin's leaving tomorrow, and we can't get him in the union that quick."

It had never occurred to either Jerry Lee or me that this man might be able to help us.

"Give me that phone and step out of the room for a minute," he said, taking off his sunglasses for the first time. "Let me see what I can get worked out."

At one point, he had called Jerry Lee back in the room, and a few minutes later, my cousin came out grinning from ear to ear.

"What happened?" I asked.

"We've got the studio, the musicians, and the union even agreed to help us with additional sessions if we need them."

When I walked into the studio, I was overwhelmed. I was about to record in the same place that had produced the greatest hit records in the world during the late 1950s. The building itself seemed filled with power.

I met Scotty Moore, who had worked with Elvis Presley, and he engineered our session at no cost. He was in the control booth getting the sound board lined up and balanced as I sat down at the piano—a big Steinway. I was so scared my hands were trembling.

As the musicians tuned their instruments and gave microphone readings to the control booth, I bowed my head and prayed. The only way I would make it through this session would be with God's help.

I prayed, "Lord, I'm not here now at somebody's invitation. I'm here with no strings attached. I'm all Yours, and I'm asking You to help me with this recording. I can't do it by myself. My total strength comes from You, and I'm believing You now for Your help and anointing."

Immediately, I sensed the anointing of the Holy Spirit on me and His presence in the studio. It took six hours to record, but when I got up from the piano, my second album was complete.

Scotty Moore slapped me on the back and said, "That's one of the best sessions I've ever been in." Then he and most of other technicians and musicians left. I stayed behind, waiting on Jerry Lee to wrap up some last minute details.

Once again, I sensed the Spirit of God moving upon me. Oddly enough, it was the same feeling I experienced four years earlier when Uncle Elmo relayed the invitation to record for Sun.

The Lord seemed to say, "Son, do you remember when I told you to trust Me?"

Of course I did. The scene was permanently etched on my mind: me standing there weeping in the broom closet of that little Assembly of God church in Ferriday asking God why I couldn't accept the offer and not fully understanding His answer.

Now, inside the studio, I heard the Lord say, "Look at this big facility. Elvis Presley was once here, but he's gone now. Johnny Cash is gone. Charlie Rich is gone. Jerry Lee is leaving. There's nothing left but a shell."

I ran through each of those big-time entertainers in my mind, and it was true. For one reason or another, they had all left. And Jerry Lee was going too, leaving for another company.

The Lord said, "You can see now that I led you right. I allowed you to use these facilities because they are the very best. But you came here on My terms, not theirs. My way is the only way because it will never bring disappointment and heartache. It always brings victory, peace, and joy."

Years before, God has saved me from making the same mistake that millions of young people make by jumping at any chance to succeed. I knew that accepting the Lord's direction for my life—even though it didn't look right at first—had proven correct. God had completely vindicated Himself in the situation.

I stood there in that studio thinking on His words to me. With tears rolling down my cheeks I said to Him, "I see, Lord. I see."

Sometime later, at a meeting I held in Pontiac, Michigan, a woman approached me after the service. She graciously introduced herself and said, "I work for Floyd Miles. He owns a record store and sponsors a program over radio station WMUZ in Detroit. I'd like to give him a copy of the record to play over the air. Perhaps it'll help you and your ministry."

"That sounds good to me," I said.

Until then, my two albums had received only minimal air play on stations that programmed gospel music. And the only venue we had for selling the records was our meetings. But that was about to change.

True to her word, the woman passed the record to Floyd Miles, and he gave it to Chuck Cossin, one of America's best known gospel disc jockeys. But Cossin took one look at the record's simple cover, called it a piece of junk, and refused to play it. "Whoever heard of Jimmy Swaggart anyway?" he said, and tossed the record aside.

Miles, who had played the record, had been touched. A month later, he came back to Cossin and asked, "Why don't you play this Swaggart record? People are coming in the store asking for it all the time. I believe it has potential."

Cossin wasn't convinced. But there came a day when he, desperate to fill air time, decided to play my record titled, *God Took Away My Yesterdays*. The radio station's switchboard lit up like a Christmas tree.

Cossin was surprised, but I was stunned. In the weeks that followed, orders for hundreds of records came pouring in from the Detroit area. Frances and I were doing all of the labeling and shipping ourselves either from the trunk of our car or from motel rooms on the road, and it was all we could to keep up with the orders coming in.

Several companies contacted me, wanting me to record, but I turned them down. Each one insisted on controlling my style of playing and singing. "None of that hallelujah stuff or talking on the records," they said. "We don't want that." So I never recorded with any of them. I could not obey the Lord and follow their orders.

It comes to me now that the Lord used this album, and the lessons around it, to change the course of my ministry.

The Spirit of the Lord touched that album, and it became a tremendous blessing to an awful lot of people all over the world. In essence, you might say that it was the first one that we made. To date, we have made well over a hundred.

Frances saw something in my music that I did not see. She knew first that it was anointed by the Holy Spirit, and she knew that it would be a blessing. I didn't think so. My answer was, "Who in the world would want to buy one of my records when they can buy all they need from people who can really sing?" However, Frances was right, as usual. There was something in the music that was a blessing, and, as stated, that something was the Lord.

I've never seen Frances lose her faith. I've seen things come and go that would kill most people, but she has consistently believed the Lord with a faith that is uncompromised. In fact, whatever we've been able to do for the Lord Jesus Christ in our efforts to touch this world for Christ, I would have to say that Frances was the biggest part of the reason for all of it being done.

A NEW HOME

I want to show you a little bit of the blessings of the Lord—how He works, and what He does.

We bought a lot in Baton Rouge and set about to build a house. In essence, it would be the first one that we ever had, outside of a little four-room place in northeast Louisiana, which was built when we first married. At any rate, I made application at one of the savings and loans for the money to construct the house. Days turned into weeks, and every time that I would go by the establishment and ask about our loan, they would say, "It's going to be ready in a short time." This went on for several weeks.

I was praying one morning in a park that was close by where we then lived. The Lord spoke to my heart and told me to go to the savings and loan and tell them we didn't want the loan anymore. In other words, I was to cancel it. I immediately wondered in my mind how we would pay for the house; but I knew the Lord had spoken, that was obvious, at least as far as I was concerned. So, I did what the Lord told me to do.

The manager of the establishment was not happy at all when I told him I was canceling my application. At any rate, that's what I did.

Our next meeting was in Detroit, Michigan, at Brightmoor Tabernacle. It was a great church, with one of the godliest pastors that I ever had the privilege to know. His name was Bond Bowman.

The Lord moved mightily in that meeting, with many people being saved. Actually, the pastor told me later that some 300 people joined the church after the meeting had concluded. At any rate, in that meeting we sold $32,000 worth of albums, which was the exact amount of the application for the loan. In other words, we were able to build the house and pay for it without owing anything, for which we give the Lord all of the glory.

I remember that when we canceled the loan, the man sarcastically asked me, "How are you going to build that house?"

My answer to him was straight and to the point. I said, "I don't know." And that was correct—at the time, I didn't know.

Some may say that with it only costing $32,000 it must not have been too much of a house, but you must remember that this was in the very early 1970s. A dollar then was worth about five times what it is today.

THE HOLY SPIRIT

In that meeting in Detroit, we had several Baptist preachers who attended the meeting many of the nights. They asked to see me, which they did.

They first of all told me, "We've never seen anything like this. When you give the altar call, we watch people run down the aisles to come to the Lord. We've never seen anything like that."

They then stated that they would like to set up a series of meetings through Michigan and Ohio. They went on to say that they would guarantee me so much money, but they had one stipulation.

"You must not preach on the Holy Spirit relative to tongues," they said. "We don't believe in that, so, we'll have to say that cannot be done."

I listened and heard them out. When they finished, I said, "Brethren, thank you so much for your offer, but there's something you don't understand. That which causes these people to run down the aisles to come to Christ is the very thing that you say you don't want—the mighty baptism with the Holy Spirit. If that is laid aside, there will be no one coming to Christ, or at least very few will. So, I'm sorry, but there's no way in the world that I can accept your offer."

Is there a heart that is waiting,
Longing for pardon today?
Hear the glad messages we bring you,
Jesus is passing this way.

Coming in love and in mercy,
Quickly now unto Him go;
Open your heart to receive Him,
Pardon and peace He'll bestow.

Listen, the Spirit is calling,
Jesus will freely forgive,
Why not this moment accept Him?
Trust in God's mercy and live.

He is so tender and loving,
He is so near you today;
Open your heart to receive Him,
While He is passing this way.

AMAZING GRACE

THE DREAM AND
THE NAME OF JESUS

"It was the beginning of being taught the power in the name of Jesus."

THE DREAM AND THE NAME OF JESUS

AS I'VE ALREADY STATED in this volume, the Lord at times reveals to us things in dreams, of which the Word of God is replete, with examples already given. If I am remembering correctly, the year was 1954. Frances and I were married in 1952, and Donnie was born in 1954. At the time of this dream, Frances was pregnant with him, possibly six or eight months along.

At that time, we were living in a little house trailer that was eight feet wide and 32 feet long, and we were glad to get it. I was just starting to preach, and the Lord would show me something in a dream that I little understood at that time. However, I would see it unfold in my life in a powerful way that was extremely negative, and yet, in some ways, it was positive.

THE DREAM

I dreamed that I was in an unfamiliar house. I was only in the front room, and as I was looking around, I saw that there were no windows in the room. As well, there was no furniture, with the room being totally barren, but with a front door that led outside.

I felt a terrible fear come over me, and my first thoughts were, "What am I doing here?" and "I've got to get out of here."

I turned to walk toward the door that led outside, and then I saw the most hideous beast that one could ever see. It was totally unlike anything on this earth. I later recognized it to be a powerful demon spirit.

It had the body of a bear and the face of a man, yet it was the eyes that literally burned with evil. When I looked at it, such fear gripped me that my legs failed me, and I fell to the floor. I was so weak that I could not respond in any manner.

I began to feel around on the floor for something with which to defend myself, as if it would have done any good. As stated, I was so weak that I could not stand. My legs would not hold me.

I was to learn from that dream that *"the weapons of our warfare are not carnal."*

Paul said, *"For though we walk in the flesh, we do not war after the flesh: (For the weapons of our warfare are not carnal, but mighty through God to the pulling down of strongholds;) Casting down imaginations, and every high thing that exalts itself against the knowledge of God, and bringing into captivity every thought to the obedience of Christ"* (II Cor. 10:3-5).

In other words, had I found something with which to defend myself, it would have done no good whatsoever. All the time this was going on, this man-beast was lumbering toward me as if to say, "I have you now," and it looked as if that would be the case.

Then, without premeditation, I shouted as loud as I could, though my voice not even above a whisper, "In the name of Jesus." That was all I said, as it was all I could say. I learned from this that the power of that name is not predicated on our personal strength, for to be sure, I had no personal strength. But even though I was terribly weak, it did not take anything away from the power of that name.

When I uttered those words—*in the name of Jesus*—that thing reeled backward, clutching its head and screaming, just like a snake that had received a death blow. It kept screaming, clutching its head, and staggering around the room. I began to gather strength, and I uttered that name again, now with much more power: "In the name of Jesus!"

As I began to rise from the floor, that beast began to fall to the floor. Whereas he had been standing over me, ready to destroy me, now I was standing over him as this demon spirit writhed in reaction on the floor, clutching its head and screaming in pain.

THE SOUND OF THE MIGHTY RUSHING WIND

I opened my mouth the third time, this time without any effort, and my voice literally boomed out, with these words reverberating off the walls in that room: "IN THE NAME OF JESUS!"

Then I heard it. I didn't see it, but I heard it.

It was the *"sound ... of a rushing mighty wind"* (Acts 2:2). It was the Holy Spirit—He came into the room and hit that thing that was writhing on the floor and knocked it out the front door!

I remember running out the door and seeing it wafting away like a leaf in the wind. What was impossible to me, considering the power of the evil spirit, was nothing for the Holy Spirit.

Remember this: We use the name of Jesus, which has tremendous power in the spirit world, but it's all made possible by the Cross of Christ. That's what gives us the authority to use that name. Incidentally, spiritual authority is never over other human beings—never. It's always authority over the powers of darkness, even over Satan himself.

That early morning hour, I awoke myself praising the Lord in other tongues. Little did I realize that this was what I would face in the coming years, but I also saw the end of the situation, and it was victory, victory, victory!

The powers of darkness are real; they're no joke. The only things that we have to combat these forces are the mighty power of the Holy Spirit and the name of Jesus. That's the reason it is such a sin and such a shame for the church to hold up something, such as humanistic psychology, as the answer to man's dilemma when there is no answer but the Cross of Christ.

THE CROSS OF CHRIST

The only answer for sin, and I mean the *only* answer, is the Cross of Christ. It was there that Jesus atoned for all sin, and I mean *all* sin—past, present, and future. As well, it was there that He triumphed over every demon spirit. The Scripture says, and I will quote from The Expositor's Study Bible, including the notes:

And you are complete in Him (the satisfaction of every spiritual want is found in Christ, made possible by the Cross), *which is the Head of all principality and power* (His Headship extends not only over the church, which voluntarily serves Him, but over all forces that are opposed to Him as well [Phil. 2:10-11]):

In whom also you are circumcised with the circumcision made without hands (that which is brought about by the Cross [Rom. 6:3-5]), *in putting off the body of the sins of the flesh by the circumcision of Christ* (refers to the old carnal nature that is defeated by the believer placing his faith totally in the Cross, which gives the Holy Spirit latitude to work):

Buried with Him in baptism (does not refer to water baptism, but rather to the believer baptized into the death of Christ, which refers to the crucifixion and Christ as our substitute, and us placing our faith exclusively in Him and what He did for us at Calvary [Rom. 6:3-4]), *wherein also you are risen with Him through the faith of the operation of God, who has raised Him from the dead.* (This does not refer to our future physical resurrection, but to that spiritual resurrection from a sinful state into divine life. We died with Him, we are buried with Him, and we rose with Him [Rom. 6:3-5], and herein lies the secret to all spiritual victory.)

And you, being dead in your sins and the uncircumcision of your flesh (speaks of spiritual death [i.e., 'separation from God'], which sin does!), *has He quickened together with Him* (refers to being made spiritually alive, which is done through being 'born again'), *having forgiven you all trespasses* (the Cross made it possible for all manner of sins to be forgiven and taken away);

Blotting out the handwriting of ordinances that was against us (pertains to the law of Moses, which was God's standard of righteousness that man could not reach), *which was contrary to us* (law is against us simply because we are unable to keep its precepts, no matter how hard we try), *and took it out of the way* (refers to the penalty of the law being removed), *nailing it to His Cross* (the law with its decrees was abolished in Christ's death, as if crucified with Him);

And having spoiled principalities and powers (Satan and all of his henchmen were defeated at the Cross by Christ atoning for all sin; sin was the legal right Satan had to hold man in captivity; with all sin atoned, he has no more legal right to hold anyone in bondage), *He* (Christ) *made a show of them openly* (what Jesus did at the Cross was in the face of the whole universe), *triumphing over them in it.* (The triumph is complete, and it was all done for us, meaning we can walk in power and perpetual victory due to the Cross.) (Col. 2:10-15).

Let us say it again: Victory over sin, the powers of darkness, and Satan himself is found only in the Cross, and I mean *only*. That means that each and every believer must have his or her faith exclusively in Christ and the Cross, and maintain it exclusively in Christ and the Cross.

ANOTHER WORD

I believe that what I am saying is based strictly on the Word of God and is a tremendous thought.

Abel placed his faith exclusively in Christ and the Cross by virtue of the sacrifice he offered. So, throughout history, beginning with Abel and on down through the many, many centuries, of all the millions who have placed their faith in Christ and the great work accomplished at Calvary, not a single one of those people has been lost. Now, think of that—not a single person.

Unfortunately, there are millions who have been lost because of placing their faith elsewhere; however, when it's placed in Christ and the atoning work of Calvary, all will make it. There may be spiritual ups and downs, there may be difficulties, and there will be many failures along the way, but when the finish line comes, by the grace of God, we will cross that line, and victory will be ours. The name of Jesus is still the most powerful name in the universe, and ever will be. When the angel of the Lord said to Joseph in a dream, *"And she* (speaking of Mary) *shall bring forth a Son, and you shall call His name Jesus: for He shall save His people from their sins"* (Mat. 1:21), he meant exactly what he said.

Let us say it again: there is no answer for sin but the Cross. We must understand that, we must know that, and we must believe that. Let me say it again: there is no answer for sin but the Cross.

Lift me up above the shadows,
Plant my feet on higher ground,
Lift me up above the clouds, Lord,
Where the pure sunshine is found;
Lift me up above my weakness,
Lift me up into Your strength,
Lift me up above the shadows,
Till I stand with You at length.

Lift me up above the shadows,
For the storms are raging high,
Lift me up, my blessed Saviour,
Let me to Your bosom fly;
There no evil thing can touch me,
Over on the shining side,
Lift me up above the shadows,
Let me evermore abide.

Lift me up above the shadows,
Out of sorrow into joy,
Lift me up above my grief, Lord,
Give me gold for my alloy,
Then, when death must claim my spirit,
And the storms of life are past,
Lift me up above the shadows,
Till in heav'n I stand at last.

Lift us up above the shadows,
When to earth you come again,
Let us be in the assembly
As Your bride to ever reign;
In Your kingdom full of glory,
With our friends we'll ever be,
Lift us up above the shadows,
There to dwell eternally.

AMAZING
GRACE

STREET CORNERS
TO STADIUMS

"In 10 minutes I preached
everything I knew—twice."

STREET CORNERS TO STADIUMS

AS I'VE ALREADY STATED in this volume, I knew from the time that I was a child that I would preach the gospel. I knew I would be involved in world evangelism, at least when I was old enough to understand what the term meant. I've learned from many years of following the Lord that He does things in His own way. He doesn't ask our permission, and He very seldom—almost never—explains Himself. Now, all of this is for a purpose and a reason. It is to increase our faith, for us to learn faith, and for us to abide by faith. That's the currency, one might say, in which God operates His economy.

The Scripture says: *"By faith Enoch was translated that he should not see death; and was not found, because God had translated him: for before his translation he had this testimony, that he pleased God. But without faith it is impossible to please Him: for he who comes to God must believe that He is, and that He is a rewarder of them who diligently seek Him"* (Heb. 11:5-6).

So, the Lord plainly says, *"But without faith it is impossible to please Him."* That's quite a statement, and it most definitely is correct. One might say that faith is the coin that spends in God's economy, and it is faith alone.

I preached my first sermon on a street corner in a little town called Mangham, Louisiana. I really don't know why I chose that place, not remembering the circumstances. It was to be the first time I would preach to an audience, yet an audience that was totally unlike a church service.

I had access in our little church in Wisner, Louisiana, to a flatbed truck that served as an excellent manner in which to have a street service. In fact, I had never participated in a street service, so I did not really know what to expect. As stated, why I chose Mangham, a little town of approximately 500 or 600 population, I don't know, but I did.

MY FIRST EFFORT

It was a Saturday afternoon, and, as most did in those days, this little country town filled with people as the farmers came in to purchase goods or whatever. At any rate, there was always a fair crowd of people in town.

I parked the big truck in front of a grocery store and actually backed it up to the sidewalk. As stated, the sidewalk was full of people.

I went into the store and asked the man if he would allow me to plug our loudspeaker system into an electrical outlet.

He looked at me and said, "Son, what are you going to do?"

I told him I was a preacher of the gospel, and we wanted to have a street service, which, more than likely, would draw quite a few people to his store. He looked at me for a moment and said, "You're welcome to use the outlet."

If I remember correctly, there was no one with me except Frances and a young girl.

I had a Sears and Roebuck amplification system, which was about all I could afford, if that. In the way of music, I had an accordion. Actually, in those days, I played an accordion constantly.

It came time to start the service, and I'll be frank with you, I was scared to death.

We started with a song, and I don't remember what song it was. As stated, I was playing my accordion and singing along with the other young lady and Frances.

In just a few moments' time, a crowd gathered. Actually, how many it was, I don't really remember but, possibly, nearly a hundred people.

We sang two or three songs, greeted the people, and then I prepared to preach. It was my first sermon.

I'll never forget the first words that I stated in that little message.

I said, "On Sept. 1, 1939, Hitler marched into Poland, which would be the start of World War II." Then I went ahead with the message.

I preached everything I knew in about five minutes, and then I started over and said it all again. Then I gave an altar call, and there was a very good response. When the service ended (it possibly only lasted about 30 minutes), I went into the store to thank the proprietor and to offer to pay him if he felt he needed something for the small amount of electricity we had used. I'll never forget what he said to me.

He said, "Son, I listened to your message, and I wish our preacher would preach like that."

He little knew that this was my very first sermon, and I was scared to death. So, when he said that, I acted like a veteran, thanked him profusely, and left.

That street service became the first of a series of Saturday services in little towns all around where we lived. As I said, it was unorthodox. It finally grew to where we had two or three musicians, and to be sure, when we began to sing and play those instruments, it would always get a crowd.

LITTLE DID I KNOW

If you had told me these simple street meetings would grow into some of the largest crusades on the face of this earth, I would have thought you were smoking something. However, that's exactly what happened.

I think of the giant citywide crusades in the largest stadiums in the world in Central and South America. I think of those in Africa and the Philippines, and I'm speaking of stadiums that seated up to 100,000 people and were packed to capacity. Had you told me in those days that this would transpire, I simply would not have believed you. I was a small-town boy who was in a little country church pastored by my dad. How in the world could that morph into that which I have just stated?

The other day one of my grandsons asked me what I remember most about those giant citywide and sometimes countrywide crusades.

I thought for a moment. It is very difficult to differentiate between so many of these great meetings that resulted in possibly the greatest harvest of souls (along with television) that mankind has ever seen. Then I remembered Santiago, Chile.

It must have been about 2 o'clock in the afternoon that Saturday, with the meeting having begun on Friday night, when President Pinochet sent for us. By us, I'm speaking of Jim Woolsey, Donnie, and me. I remarked to Jim that we really didn't have time to do this, but he told me that we didn't have any choice. They picked us up in a helicopter and took us to one of the retreats where the president was then staying.

We spent about two hours with him, with the helicopter then taking us back. As we were coming back into Santiago, we passed right over the giant stadium, and even then (about 5 o'clock in the afternoon), it was packed to capacity.

I don't really remember what I preached that Saturday night, but I do remember that we had an altar call that probably resulted in the largest altar call that has ever been given.

The manager of the stadium was accustomed to big crowds, for they played soccer at this stadium. I had no way to count the people, but he related to one of my people that it was approximately 28,000 people who responded to the altar call that Saturday night. No, all of those people didn't get saved. How many gave their hearts to Christ, I really don't know. Some of them just wanted prayer, but at any rate, that many responded.

THIS I DO KNOW

In almost every church in these countries, you will find people there who gave their hearts to Christ in those giant crusades, or else, through our telecasts, which, at that time, aired all over Central and South America.

I remember getting a letter from a girl, who had given it to one of our people, and then it was passed on to me.

She stated that she was in that meeting that night in Santiago, that is, if I can rightly remember the city and the stadium.

She told me in the letter that she had been a member of Shining Path, which was a notorious communist organization that was trying to overthrow the government in all of these countries. She went on to state how she really did not know why she went to the meeting that night, but she did.

At any rate, this girl was one of that 28,000, that is, if Santiago was the city. She gave her heart to Christ and told me, "Brother Swaggart, my world changed that night. It changed from a life of hate to a life of love, all because of the Lord Jesus Christ." How many untold thousands of letters have we received as it regards the same identical testimony!

SAN SALVADOR, EL SALVADOR

Along with airing the telecast in that beautiful little Central American country, we also built some 34 schools in San Salvador, plus in other areas of that country. These schools would take care of children up and through grade six. Each school handled anywhere from 500 to 1,000 kids. We gave them a hot meal each day at noon, plus we paid for the teachers, etc. Overall, we built 144 schools in various countries in Central and South America, plus Haiti. Those were in addition to the Bible schools and churches, which we built by the scores.

I was speaking with a lawyer in El Salvador, who had been the legal counsel for the president of that country. He related to me how that during a recent earthquake they had, which we were very much aware of, a library of books fell over on him and hurt his back greatly. The doctors did all they could for him, but all to no avail. He went on to relate to me how the pain was almost unbearable.

When we went to El Salvador for the crusade, the crowds were gigantic. Actually, they had to close the stadium about an hour before service time because there was no more room for the people. At any rate, this lawyer walked out of his office, hailed a cab, and told the driver to take him to the stadium. The driver told him, "There's no point in going; they've closed all the doors and gates, and they have no more room for anyone else."

He heard the driver say these words, pondered a moment, and then told him, "Go ahead and take me anyway."

When he arrived at the stadium, it was exactly as the cab driver had stated—there were hundreds, if not thousands of people outside, hoping for a way to get in. He said that he walked up to the giant wall that surrounded the stadium and just started walking around it. Miracle of miracles, he found an opening and let himself in. There was no place to sit down, so he had to stand, and the pain in his back was so bad that he could hardly bear it.

HEALING

The service started and as that massive crowd was singing a chorus, this man said that he felt something start at the top of his head and go down his back. "It was like a ball of fire," he said. Instantly, the pain stopped, and he said, "Brother Swaggart, I knew that I was healed," and so he was, by the grace of God.

Incidentally, as it regarded the crusades in those particular countries, the Lord told me that I should encourage the people to look to the Lord Jesus Christ. He told me to tell them, "Don't look to the government and don't look to America, but look to Christ." That's what I did in preaching message after message. Hebrews 12:2 says, *"Looking unto Jesus the author and finisher of our faith."*

As an aside, even though our dear brother who experienced the miracle of healing had been prayed for many times in his church, it was all to no avail. And yet, standing in this vast assembly with no one to lay hands on him and no one to anoint him with oil, he was instantly healed by the power of God. No, it doesn't mean that these other things are wrong, for they aren't. It just means that the Lord has a way of doing things, which is never our way. Why the Lord waited for this particular time to heal our brother, I cannot answer that. I just thank God that this man experienced a miracle. When he gave me his testimony, tears filled his eyes, and no wonder.

Only the Lord knows the vast number of people who gave their hearts to Christ in those crusades, as well as those who were healed by the power of God and set free from alcohol, drugs, etc. The Holy Spirit said, "Preach Jesus," and that's exactly what I did, which resulted in a tremendous harvest.

PANAMA

The following is one of the most gripping stories of the grace of God that I think can be found any place. It began in the mid-1960s in the great city of Colón, Panama in Central America. It concluded, or at least our part of it did, in Panama City, Panama, in the mid-1980s—a timeframe of some 20 years or more. The missionary we were working with had set out to build a church in Colón. He rented a theater in the heart of the city and asked us to come preach a meeting to get the effort started, which we did.

For whatever reason, Frances was not with me on this particular trip. At any rate, it was a Saturday night, and there was an excellent crowd in the building; the Spirit of God moved in a mighty way. I still remember the message that I preached titled, "More Abundant Life."

When I gave the altar call, there was a good response, but something happened that set it apart from anything else.

THE MIRACLE

As I was exhorting the people, and I speak of those who had come to be saved, all of a sudden a young man made his way to the stage and then to the platform. As he got closer, it was obvious that he was a cripple. He was dragging his right leg behind him with some effort.

He walked up to me, at least as best he could walk, reached into the tunic of his coat, and pulled out the biggest revolver I'd ever seen. I can't tell you how I felt. Here was a man standing with a gun in his hand some two or three feet from me.

What did I do? To be frank, I just stood there breathing a prayer.

The man took his gun, laid it on the pulpit, and told me his story. He said:

Brother Swaggart, one year ago today, a man in Panama City purposely ran over me with a car, and I lost my right leg. Consequently, I am a cripple—only half a man—and that's the way I've had to live the last year. I had made up my mind that I was going to kill him. I purchased a gun, and there it is on the pulpit. I was going to go to Panama City today, for I know where he is, and I was going to take his life. But my mother was celebrating her birthday, and when I asked her what she wanted, she told me, 'I only want one thing, and that is for you to go to church with me tonight.' She didn't know anything about my intentions of going to Panama City to kill this man. I know now that it was the Lord who moved upon her to ask what she did. She wouldn't take no for an answer, so I finally consented. I put off killing the man until the next few days. I'm here tonight, and I have given my heart and life to Jesus Christ. I'm going to Panama City in a few days, but not to kill the man. Yes, I'm going to find him. But I'm going to tell him what Jesus Christ has done for me.

As stated, this was one of the most remarkable stories, but it's not over yet. Some 20 years later, we preached a citywide crusade in beautiful Panama City, Panama. That stadium seated, I suppose, some 35,000 or more, and every service it was packed to capacity.

The first service was on a Friday night. As stated, the crowd was great, and the operation of the Holy Spirit was even better.

As I closed out my message, I told the story that I've just related to you, but little did I expect what was about to happen. As I asked the people to bow their heads and started the altar call, all of a sudden I saw a big man coming across the infield. He was dragging his leg, waving his arms, and shouting something, but I couldn't make it out as the platform was far from the bleachers. But as he got closer, his words began to come through. He was shouting, "I am the man! I am the man!"

He made his way to the platform, and I remember walking down from the stage, putting my arms around him, and saying, "You mean you're the man that I was talking about tonight?" He said, "Yes, Brother Swaggart. I'm now preaching the gospel. Actually, I'm a youth pastor at a large church here in Panama City, and it all began that Saturday night when I gave my heart to Christ and my world changed."

BUENOS AIRES, ARGENTINA

This was a different situation than we had ever encountered. In preparing for these giant crusades, we always sent people ahead to take care of all of the duty problems, along with customs, etc. In those days we had to take everything with us as there was nothing locally that you could obtain that would be needed.

In other words, we had to take all of the television equipment, all of the sound equipment, and all of the big generators in case the power went out. When you consider that we were covering a stadium that seated upwards of 100,000 people, the amount of sound equipment was staggering. Actually, we always rented a 747 cargo plane in those days, and it would be jammed to capacity with equipment.

We did the same thing with Buenos Aires; however, we ran into a problem.

The customs officials took our equipment, locked it into a side room, which was almost as big as a landing field for an airplane, and wouldn't allow the equipment to be released unless we paid them $50,000 (if I remember the amount correctly).

Our people worked day and night trying to get the equipment released, explaining that we had already taken care of all of this. Actually, this was the first time we had ever run into anything of this nature.

HOW GOD MOVED

The pastors in the city had hosted a breakfast that was to be conducted in the hotel where we were staying. It was all in honor of the crusade.

Of course, I went to that meeting that morning with a heavy heart. I was very concerned, not knowing what we were going to do simply because we couldn't get the equipment released. We had tried everything.

When I arrived in the ballroom, it was packed to capacity. I was told that the people present were some of the most influential people in Buenos Aires. Actually, the ambassador from the United States to Argentina was one of the guests.

I sensed early on a gentle tugging of the Holy Spirit, encouraging me to preach on the infilling of the Holy Spirit. Now, please understand that I was in no way reluctant to do what the Lord wanted; I just wanted to make sure it was the Lord.

My mind said that these people didn't know anything about the Holy Spirit. They wouldn't know what I was talking about.

Nevertheless, the pressure became harder and heavier. Finally, I told my translator that I was changing the message and gave him the Scripture that I felt the Lord wanted me to use. As is usual, the Holy Spirit was right.

A MOVE OF GOD

The Spirit of God moved that morning like waves across that audience of people. Men and women were openly sobbing and weeping as the presence of God touched their hearts and touched their lives. I have every confidence that many needs were met that early morning hour, all because of the presence of the Lord.

When I was about ready to leave and go back to the room, a lady, stylishly dressed, walked up to me and said,

"Brother Swaggart, I understand that you're having problems getting your equipment out of customs."

I looked at her. Stains of mascara had streaked down her face as she had wept and sobbed before the Lord. She was a very lovely lady, possibly in her 50s.

"How did you know about this?" I asked.

I don't really remember her answer, but she then said to me, "Perhaps I can help you get that equipment released."

I looked at her and wondered how in the world such could be, considering that our people had spent the last two days, almost day and night, trying to get this thing done all to no avail.

I said to her, "How?"

She said, "Brother Swaggart, my brother is the president."

I looked at her and said, "The president of what?"

She smiled and said, "Brother Swaggart, my brother is the president of Argentina."

I knew then that she most definitely could help. The fact is that our equipment was released that afternoon in time for the beginning of the meeting. Look what the Lord has done! As the old song says, "The Lord knows the way through the wilderness, and all we have to do is follow."

LIBERIA, WEST AFRICA

The city was Monrovia, situated on the ocean, and that part of the world is infested with demon spirits. It is to such a degree as to be unimaginable, at least as we think of such here in America.

As I went to the stadium each night, witch doctors lined the road that we traveled, trying to put curses on us.

And yet, people came from many miles away to be in the meetings. Some of them walked almost all day long in order to be in the service. That's a hunger for God that the Lord will never let fall by the wayside.

Once again, it was a Saturday night. The stadium, which seated about 35,000 or 40,000, was brand-new, having just been built by the Chinese, and it was packed to capacity. Actually, we were one of the first events to be conducted in that structure.

That Saturday night, when the service was turned to me, there was a yipping—like dogs yipping. It began to swell out across the vast congregation until it became a roar. As mentioned, the stadium was packed to capacity. I knew this was demon spirits that were trying to stop the service. That meant that there were hundreds and hundreds, even thousands, of people in that stadium that night who were demon-possessed.

I stood as close to the microphone as I could and asked the engineer to turn up the volume as high as he could. Then I stated, "In the name of Jesus, I command you to shut up."

It was like you had cut off running water from a faucet. Instantly, the noise ceased and all of the yipping stopped. There were no more disturbances in that service. It was the most instant moving of the Holy Spirit in such a capacity that I had ever experienced or witnessed.

Let us all understand that there is power in that name, and it is power that is unimaginable for its glory and its strength.

HAITI

This ministry—Jimmy Swaggart Ministries—built some 38 schools in the little island country of Haiti. These schools took care of approximately 500 or 600 children each, and went through the sixth grade, at least most of them did, with a few going all the way through high school.

At any rate, the first school that we built sat almost immediately in front of the home of one of the most notorious witch doctors in Haiti. Actually, I interviewed his wife and asked her why they offered up sacrifices to demon spirits. Her reply was very interesting. She said, "We do what we do because we are fearful of what the spirits will do to us if it's not done."

We built a church right beside the school, and this witch doctor's 11-year-old son was one of the first to give his heart to Christ.

What I'm about to relate did not pertain to that particular witch doctor. It does pertain to *the* most notorious witch doctor—we were told—in Haiti.

We had built a very large church in a certain part of Haiti, and it was pastored by a very godly young man, who was seeing great things done for the Lord. One particular day he ran into this witch doctor on the street. Due to the fact that many people were getting saved and no longer seeking the services of these witch doctors, it made these individuals very angry. This witch doctor stopped my pastor friend on the street and began to berate him.

He told him, "In 30 days you and Jimmy Swaggart will be dead. I'm putting a curse on you, and so you have about 30 days to live, if that."

My friend looked at the witch doctor and said, "Your curse be placed back on your own head. In 30 days, neither I nor Jimmy Swaggart will be dead, but *you* will be dead."

Before the 30-day limit had passed, that witch doctor dropped dead from a heart attack.

JOHANNESBURG, SOUTH AFRICA

I have been to South Africa some five or six times, I suppose. Donnie has been there nearly 30 times, preaching all over that vast land.

The crusade in Ellis Park Stadium was one of the first integrated events in South Africa. I had visited the year before and not everyone had been allowed to attend that meeting. So when I was invited back, I agreed to minister under the condition that anyone, regardless of race, could attend. This historic integration was captured in our footage of that 1981 crusade, where many wonderful things happened.

What I'm about to relate is, I think, one of the greatest. Actually, there is no miracle greater than a soul being saved.

That night, and I think it was Saturday, a young African came into the stadium, thinking it was a soccer match. Actually, he was very much inebriated. He found a seat somewhere high up in the bleachers and sat down there. Never having been in a service of this nature in his life, he was wondering what in the world was taking place there.

That night during the service, the Holy Spirit sobered up that young African and, when the altar call was given, he was one among the many who came. I did not see him, did not know him, and had no idea what had taken place in his life. But that night he gave his heart and life to Jesus Christ. Only the story does not end there.

About a year or two later, Donnie was in South Africa in meetings. Early in the morning, he heard a knock at his motel door. He got up, turned on the light, and opened the door. There stood this young black African. Donnie did not know him but was to soon learn some wonderful things.

The young man immediately opened up the conversation by asking, "How is Daddy Jimmy and Mama Frances?"

"Do you know my mother and dad?" Donnie asked.

The young man then told Donnie his story—how he had been saved out of a life of drunkenness. Then he took out from under his arm a Bible, which Donnie said was the biggest Bible he had ever seen.

He told Donnie, "I'm preaching the gospel now, with my life having been saved from drunkenness and a life of crime." Then he said, "I give all the glory to the Lord Jesus Christ."

That's the power of the gospel, and nothing will ever remotely compare with that. It is the answer to man's dilemma, and it is the *only* answer.

DETROIT, MICHIGAN

We were in the giant Cobo Arena in Detroit for a citywide crusade. I preached my first meeting in Detroit at Bond Bowman's church, Brightmoor Tabernacle. We had a tremendous meeting, and as previously stated in this volume, there were more than 300 people who joined the church after the meetings were concluded.

So, we were to have great crowds at Cobo, which was an arena seating, I suppose, of about 15,000—maybe a little more.

Before the service, Donnie came to the room where Frances and I were staying.

"Dad, we've got a problem," he said. "The teamsters union has served notice on us that in order for us to open tonight, we're going to have to pay them $30,000. You might better go over to the coliseum. Possibly you can talk some sense into them."

I walked over to the coliseum with Donnie inasmuch as the hotel in which we were staying was right next door.

Actually, it was only one man who was demanding this type of money. He said that unless we paid it, the meetings would not begin that night, or any night for that matter.

When I walked into the meeting, I saw this man who was causing all the problems standing nearby.

Immediately, another man appeared, looked at me, and said, "Brother Swaggart, is that you?" He stated that he was so glad we were in Detroit, and if there was anything he could do for us, we were to just let him know.

So I mentioned to him, "This man over here says we have got to pay $30,000, or we will not open tonight." I told him how that we had already taken care of all the expenses as we always did with each crusade.

He walked over to the man demanding the money and said, "What are you doing trying to hold up this preacher?"

The man made some type of wisecrack back at him and then, all of a sudden—actually, in a flash—my friend grabbed this man's shirt collar, slammed him up against a concrete pole, and asked, "How much are you charging?"

The man gave some number, and my friend kept slamming his head up against that concrete pole until I thought he was going to do some serious damage. Finally, it got down to $30, and I told him to just leave the man; we'd pay the $30. So, it had come from $30,000 down to just $30. (Incidentally, that man who had caused the initial problem quickly sneaked out, to be sure.)

"Brother Swaggart, if you need anything else, just let me know," this man, still unknown to me, said.

I thanked him profusely and when he started to walk away, I asked who he was. He gave his name, but that did not mean anything. The people with whom I was speaking and who had observed all the proceedings said, "Brother Swaggart, that man is Jimmy Hoffa's personal body guard."

I'll always thank the Lord that He sent that man at the last moment. He saved us a considerable amount of money, as would be obvious. I may not have approved of his tactics, but I was finding it very difficult to reprimand him in any way. Of that, you can be sure.

We had a similar scene in Toronto, Ontario, Canada.

TORONTO, ONTARIO

We were setting up the equipment that Friday morning to start the crusade that night. We were in the Maple Leaf

Gardens arena. I suppose it seats 15,000 to 20,000 people. It's where the Toronto Maple Leafs hockey team plays. We had the same kind of problem with people wanting to hold us up, trying to force us to pay a large sum of money, which we did not have.

At any rate, I was standing there talking with a man about this, trying to get him to understand, when a white-headed gentleman walked up.

Just like before, this man said, "Brother Swaggart, we're so very glad to have you in Ontario. Is there anything I can do for you?"

I didn't know what good it would do, but I spoke to him and said, "Yes, we need some help as it regards a problem we're facing. This man wants to charge us money, which we really do not owe. He's telling us that if we don't pay it, we will not start the meeting tonight."

The white-headed gentleman walked over, tapped the other man on the shoulder, and asked him to step aside with him, which he did. In about three or four minutes, the gentleman came back and said, "Brother Swaggart, everything is all right now. You don't owe anything."

As he turned to walked away, he said that if I needed any more help to just let him know. There was a large crowd there, so I asked some people standing nearby who that man was. They gave me his name, and I found that he owned that arena, plus the Toronto Maple Leafs hockey team, and just about half of everything else in that great city. Needless to say, we didn't have any more problems.

ANOTHER MEETING IN DETROIT

At a later time, we were in Detroit in the same arena—Cobo—for a one-night rally. During the years, we had seen literally hundreds of people brought to Christ in the Detroit area, and I was personally looking forward to that service. Once again, the crowd was fantastic; they had a high expectation of the service.

If I remember correctly, Frances was not with me at that time. I don't know why, but she wasn't.

The service began that night with praise and worship, and there was a tremendous moving of the Spirit as the Lord anointed me, powerfully, to preach.

When the service ended, I stepped down from the platform to go back to the dressing room. I was met by a mob of people, but there was one man who stood out. He was a black brother and he must have stood 6 feet 6 inches tall, weighing approximately 250 pounds—all bone and muscle.

He grabbed me and picked me up as if I were a rag doll—my feet not even touching the floor—and then gave me one of the most astounding testimonies one could ever hear.

He told me how that he had been a member of the Black Panther Party and was a man who was filled with hate, especially for white people.

He told how he had staggered home drunk on a Saturday night, turned on the TV set, and fell into a drunken sleep on the couch. He was awakened that Sunday morning by the television, and our program was on.

He lurched up from the couch to turn the TV channel because he hated white people, but something stopped him— something that was greater than he was. He sat back down on the couch and began to listen, and then, for the first time in his life, he sensed the presence of God.

He went on to tell me how he had not shed a tear since he was a little boy, but that morning he found himself weeping.

When I gave the altar call, he dropped down beside the couch and repeated the sinner's prayer with me, and his whole world changed.

He said, "Brother Swaggart, my life is totally different now. Love has replaced hate. Now I'm preaching the gospel of Jesus Christ, and I have a story to tell."

Oh, yes, he does!

As I continued through the crowd of people in the arena that night, I shook hands with scores of people. When I got to the door that led into the hallway, a young lady stopped me. I didn't know who she was.

She looked at me and said, "Brother Swaggart, you don't remember me, do you?"

I didn't want to embarrass her, but I didn't remember her. She pointed to her eye, and then, all of a sudden, it began to come back to me.

She said, "My eye is still completely healed, with no trace of blindness left."

Let me tell you what happened.

We were at Brightmoor Tabernacle, and it was a Friday night, I think. When the service ended, this young lady walked up to me. At that time, she was 14 years old. She had on an old raggedy coat that was not even worth throwing away, but she still wore it every night because, being January, it was cold.

I found out later that she had hitchhiked to service every night, which was a very dangerous thing for a young girl to do. But she was so hungry for God that she didn't want to miss a service; she saw in the Lord that which would change her life.

When the service ended, she walked up to me and said, "Does Jesus Christ still heal the sick, even opening blinded eyes?"

I looked at her and said, "Yes, young lady, He still does."

"Do you think that He will open my blinded eye?"

I asked her which eye it was. If I remember correctly, she pointed to her right eye. "You mean you can't see anything out of it?" I asked.

She said, "No. It's totally blind."

At any rate, I prayed for her. Now don't misunderstand; it was not my faith that performed this miracle; it was hers.

A minute or two later, Bruce Gunn, who was one of the associate pastors at Brightmoor Tabernacle, shouted out across the room, "Brother Swaggart, there has been a miracle!"

He then walked up with this young lady and said to me, "The Lord has opened her blinded eye."

I'll be frank with you, I don't know how I felt. I was shaking all over as I said to her, "Honey, put your hand over your good eye," and I held up one or two fingers, whatever it was, and asked her how many fingers she could see out of the eye that had been blind. And she, with a big smile on her face, gave the correct number, not once, but several times. I knew she was healed. But, as stated, it was not my faith that did it. It was her faith.

Sometimes when misgivings darken the day,
And faith's light I cannot see;
I ask my dear Lord to brighten the way,
And He whispers sweet peace to me.

I could not go on without Him I know,
The world would overwhelm my soul;
For I could not see the right way to go,
When temptations over me roll.

I trust Him through faith, by faith hold His hand,
And sometimes my faith is weak,
And then when I ask Him to take command,
It seems that I hear Him speak.

He speaks in a still, small voice, we are told,
A voice that dispels all fear;
And when I'm in doubt, or troubled in soul,
That still small voice I can hear.

He whispers sweet peace to me,
He whispers sweet peace to me,
When I am cast down in spirit and soul,
He whispers sweet peace to me.

AMAZING GRACE

CHAPTER 10

DIVINE PROTECTION

"What we experienced—and will experience to a greater degree in coming campmeetings—is what the modern church, our nation, and the world desperately needs."

DIVINE PROTECTION

AS IT REGARDS MEETINGS in churches presently, there aren't many that go longer than a weekend—usually Friday, Saturday, and Sunday.

When Frances and I began back in the 1950s, all meetings, at least for us, lasted some two weeks. Ours averaged some four weeks in duration, and that was every night except Saturday.

The longest revival that I preached was a nine-week meeting at Brightmoor Tabernacle in Detroit, Michigan. However, that meeting, if I remember correctly, was only Friday, Saturday, and Sunday of each week.

In those days, and possibly lasting up until the turn of the 21st century, most all of districts of the Assemblies of God, with which we were associated, had yearly campmeetings. However, I do not recall the Louisiana district ever having a campmeeting, at least when I was preaching those types of meetings. So, the first campmeeting that I was ever in, I was privileged to preach at the night services. Incidentally, it lasted about a week or two in duration.

Only preachers who were seasoned veterans of the Word were asked to preach these meetings, at least the night services where the biggest crowds by far were attending. Actually, I don't remember the first camp that I preached. I do remember that I preached the Illinois camp some 11 times. The preachers who preached the morning services when I was there were renowned—names such as C.M. Ward, etc. These were giants of the faith who would be hard to be duplicated presently.

For some reason, I wanted to preach campmeetings even before, as stated, I had ever been in one. So I asked the Lord to open the doors, which He definitely did, and I preached camps all over the nation. Actually, as far as I know, I was the youngest campmeeting preacher at that time, and possibly ever, at least in the Assemblies of God. All of them stand out, but one camp, in particular, because of a certain thing that happened.

THE FLOOD

It was the Ohio District of the Assemblies of God. We were having a great camp. I did something that most campmeeting preachers never did, and that was to preach a salvation message every Sunday night, which had the biggest crowd. We saw a moving of the Holy Spirit that resulted in many people being saved.

At any rate, we were having a great camp in Ohio when a storm erupted. If I remember correctly, it was on a Saturday night.

We were staying in a house right beside a small river just a very short distance from the tabernacle. It rained so hard that night that Frances, Donnie, and I were awakened by water coming into the house. That's how bad it was.

We got what little stuff we could into the car, but water was already up to the seats, and the car wouldn't start.

The next morning we were trying to get back into the house (at least I was) to retrieve whatever we could when I was almost swept under the house by the receding waters. Had it not been for a dear brother standing nearby, I would have drowned. He grabbed me and held on for dear life.

When that camp ended, we went to our next meeting in Fort Worth, Texas. On the first Sunday morning we were there, a dear elderly lady walked up to me and said, "Brother Swaggart, did you have any difficulty in the last few days concerning water or almost drowning?"

I was startled when she said that; I had not mentioned the situation in this meeting. I looked at her and said, "Do you know what happened to us?"

She had no knowledge of what had happened, but she said that the Spirit of God awakened her days earlier and told her, "Get up and pray for Jimmy Swaggart. Satan is going to try to kill him this morning." She went on to say how the Holy Spirit had warned her that it was drowning that the Evil One was trying to bring to pass.

I knew that she had absolutely no knowledge of what had taken place, but she stood before me on that Sunday morning in that church in Fort Worth and described exactly what had happened to me. And, as she spoke, I began to realize how powerful the Holy Spirit actually is.

AN AIRPLANE

I had another incident that was very similar to that one, although of a different nature.

We closed out a crusade in Virginia Beach, Virginia. We had a great meeting, with thousands of people in attendance. Many were saved, and many were baptized with the Holy Spirit.

In those days, we were flying our own plane. It was one of the old DC-3s. It was a sturdy plane and seated about 12 people, but it was slow. Actually, it would only fly about 150 miles per hour. As we left Virginia Beach that night, the weather was perfect, but little did we realize what was about to happen.

I suppose we were about two hours out from Virginia Beach on our way to Baton Rouge when we ran into bad weather.

I was exhausted from the meetings, and I had laid down on the floor and had actually gone to sleep. Suddenly, I was awakened by turbulence and immediately recognized that we were in the midst of a storm.

It was raining so hard that I couldn't see the lights that flashed on and off on the plane's wingtips. I looked through the cockpit door, and I saw the radar swinging wildly back and forth—it was out of order. I heard our pilot, Greg Wieser, calling out, "Mayday, Mayday," and I realized that we were in trouble.

The left engine began to miss. It's a peculiar feeling to be in an airplane in the midst of a storm when an engine begins to miss—the whole plane vibrates.

AN AIRLINER

As stated, Greg was calling out for help. Without our radar, we couldn't tell if we were flying into the worst part of the storm or not. It was a perilous situation.

Through the crackling static, I heard someone responding back to Greg's distress call. It was the pilot of a 737 passenger jet.

He told Greg, "I can catch you on my radar, and I'm going to slow my plane down to just above stall speed, and I think I can guide you through the storm."

He gave Greg the vectors and stayed on the air as long as he could, and we made it through this near tragedy.

Our next meeting was in Lakeland, Florida. Once again, I had not had an opportunity to say anything to anybody about what had transpired on our flight the week before.

In the meeting, I was sitting on the platform with some other preachers while the host pastor of the crusade addressed the people. The dear brother seated beside me leaned over and said, "Brother Swaggart, did you have a problem of any sort last Sunday night?"

I looked at him and said, "Yes, we were in the midst of a storm in our plane and almost didn't make it."

He told me how the Lord had awakened him and his wife and said, "Jimmy Swaggart is in trouble. Get up and pray."

Once again, that was the Holy Spirit.

What a mighty God we serve,
What a mighty God we serve,
Angels bow before Him,
Heaven and earth adore Him,
What a mighty God we serve.

BACK TO OHIO

Getting back to the campmeeting where I almost drowned, we lost everything in that flood—our car, all of our clothes (and I mean *all* of our clothes)—everything.

Believe it or not, I borrowed a pair of trousers from a lady. They came almost up to my knees. Not being able to shave because of having lost all of that paraphernalia, well, I'm not going to try to tell you how I looked.

Frances and I went to a pastor's home, who was a good friend of ours. Now remember, that was a Sunday, and all the stores were closed, meaning that I could not purchase anything to wear. Still, I had to have a car, so Monday morning I went with the pastor to a dealership, and I can't tell you how I looked. As stated, I hadn't shaved in two or three days, and my hair looked like the wild man of Borneo; I had no way to comb it.

At the dealership, I picked out a car, and, of course, the owner of the establishment kept staring at me. I told him how that we had been in a flood, but he didn't seem to understand.

He asked me if I wanted to test drive the car and I said, "No, that won't be necessary." He called the bank on which I had written the check. Banks normally check your records to see if everything is alright concerning whomever it might be. This was a small-town bank, and I knew the manager very well, so he didn't bother about checking. He just told the man the check was good.

I went the next morning and purchased some clothes, as did Frances, and then the pastor took us over to get the car. When I walked into the man's office, I don't think he recognized me. I'd had a chance to shave, my hair was combed, and I had on some clothes that were totally different than what I had worn the day before.

Once again I explained to the owner what had happened. He sat there and smiled and said, "I was very concerned that you were stealing my car."

I'll admit that I had looked the part, but I was no thief, just a vagabond traveler at this particular stage.

Getting back to campmeetings, I don't recall the last camp that I preached. I do know that during those years the Lord gave us some great services with many people being saved and many being baptized with the Holy Spirit.

All that thrills my soul is Jesus,
Every day and every hour;
Jesus and His free salvation,
Jesus and His mighty power.

His is love beyond all knowledge,
His is grace beyond degree,
Mercy higher than the heavens,
Deeper than the deepest sea.

Every need His hand supplieth,
Every good in Him I see;
And the strength He gives His weak ones,
Is sufficient unto me.

What a wonderful redemption!
Never can a mortal know,
How my sin, though red like crimson
Can be whiter than the snow.

In yon everlasting city,
With the ransomed I will sing,
And forever and forever,
Praise and glorify the King.

All that thrills my soul is Jesus,
He is more than life to me;
And the fairest of ten thousands,
In my blessed Lord I see.

AMAZING GRACE

"I never dreamed I would ever be on radio."

RADIO

IT WAS 1968. I was preaching meetings all over the country at that time, and the Lord was doing great things. Then, in prayer, I began to feel in my spirit that He wanted me to go on radio. I mentioned it to Frances, and she felt the same way that I did.

My knowledge of radio was very limited. I had been on radio a few times in traveling from church to church, but we were now speaking of a 15-minute program each day, Monday through Friday. For one thing, that's quite expensive. Where would the money come from? To be frank, even though I definitely felt led of the Lord to do this, there was a fear in my heart about the situation simply because of my lack of knowledge in this area.

I went to Houston, Texas, to a place that sold the equipment I would need to get started. I was told that this store had the right equipment, but I didn't even know enough about it to be able to tell the man what I needed. I had to ask for his guidance and help, which he gave.

After I came back home, I contacted an engineer in Baton Rouge and had him put the equipment together.

THE FIRST PROGRAM

The first program was aired Jan. 1, 1969 over a station in Atlanta, Georgia. Immediately we took on two other stations: KFMK in Houston, Texas, and a station in Beckley, West Virginia.

Why I chose those three, I really don't know. I'm sure at the time there was a reason, but it presently slips my mind.

The program over the three respective stations mentioned above had been on the air about 90 days. Our response had been almost nonexistent. I did not realize then that I would have to stay on a station sometimes as long as two years before I would be able to develop an audience. All I knew was that I was running out of money fast.

I was continuing to conduct crusades across America. I was using every dime of the money I could get from the crusades to pay the radio time. I have always been a stickler for paying bills. My dad taught me to pay what I owed when it was due. Consequently, we have developed that particular practice all through the years. We now have the reputation for being prompt in paying our bills in the radio and television business. That makes me very happy. I always feel that a Christian should conduct his business to provide an example of honesty in everything that is done.

When I think of the tremendous expense we have today, the sum of $15 or $20 a day at that time seems a mere pittance. However, then it was a mountain. I soon spent almost everything I could get my hands on, and I could see nothing but bankruptcy if the situation continued as it was. The mail response was almost nothing, and I really did not know what to do. I sought God's face earnestly. I knew He had told me to do this, yet what was the problem?

CRISIS POINT

Around this particular time, I was engaged to preach a crusade in Louisville, Kentucky. I had almost made up my mind to go off the air. I felt our response was so small there was no point in continuing. I also fought the blackest spirit of depression I think I have ever experienced. Frances did not go with me to this particular meeting. I called her about the first part of the crusade and told her I had made up my mind—I was definitely going to cancel *The Campmeeting Hour* and go off the air.

Frances is the type of person who does not give up easily. Actually, that is an understatement. She, too, strongly felt it was God's will that we be there, yet, neither one of us knew the answer. We just knew that we were running out of money. It seemed to be a bottomless pit, and there was no way out. She told me her feelings: she thought I should stay on the air. She even went so far as to say we would sell the furniture in the house, if necessary, to stay on. I don't think I will ever forget that statement. If I could sum up the word *dedication*, that would be it. Nevertheless, I brushed aside her remark (even though it went deep into my heart) and told her my mind was made up I was writing the stations and canceling the program.

I set up my little portable typewriter on the side of the bed in that Holiday Inn and wrote the three respective letters to the three stations canceling *The Campmeeting Hour*. As I typed the words on the paper, many times I could hardly see how to type for the tears in my eyes. I knew I was doing wrong, but I didn't know what else to do. I had sought God incessantly over the problem, but it was seemingly to no avail. I was running out of money. Whenever the stations sent their bills, I knew I had to pay them. At this particular time, I had no money to pay the bills, so what was I to do? To me, there was no alternative but cancel.

After I mailed the letters, I slept very little the next week. In that crusade, night after night I would preach. God gave us a great outpouring of His Holy Spirit. Many lives were changed. I would come back after service totally exhausted and walk the floor in my motel room many times until daylight. I would lay prone on the floor sobbing as the Holy Spirit would tell me over and over again, "What you have done has not pleased Me. This is not My will."

THE HAND OF THE LORD

To show you how the Holy Spirit works, what I'm about to say was and still is beautiful to me because I know the Lord orchestrated it.

I found out later that when the three station managers received my letters of cancellation, all three of them took my 15 minutes of scheduled air time and explained to the people what I had said. They stated that this program should not be cancelled, and if the people wanted it to remain, they should write me a letter and send an offering, if possible. Each of the three station managers did the same thing without any knowledge of what the others were doing.

In fact, the dear brother at the station in Atlanta, Georgia, was Baptist. He told his audience, "Jimmy Swaggart and I disagree on some points of doctrine, but I do know this program is needed, and I want you to help keep it on the air." I will always be grateful to this dear Baptist brother.

As mentioned, the other two managers—Hardy Brundage in Houston (who later managed two of our stations), plus the brother in Beckley—did the same thing.

IN REVIVAL

The next morning at about 10 o'clock, Frances called me. I could tell by her voice that she was very excited.

She said, "You won't believe what happened! The doorbell rang, and I went to the door, and the postman was standing there, saying, 'What do you want me to do with this?'"

He was asking her what he should do with a huge mail sack that had some 900 letters in it. Yes, I said 900 letters—all from listeners encouraging us to stay on the air. And many of the letters, if not all, included offerings.

I wish I could say it was my faith that did this, but as I look back, I cannot be honest and say that. I think it was Frances' faith and the men who were over the stations. I doubt that they really knew what they were doing as far as the significance was concerned. God used them to defeat the powers of darkness and enable *The Campmeeting Hour* to stay on the air, bringing blessing to many people.

NOW WE BEGIN TO GROW

We immediately began to add other stations. God began to bless. He began to touch the hearts of people to help support the program. Lives began to be blessed. We began to receive so many letters from people telling us how the program had answered so many questions for them. Scores of people began to receive a hunger for the mighty infilling of the Holy Spirit. Others began to launch out in faith in deeper waters in the Spirit and receive from the Lord as they had never received before.

We began to take on new stations: WBIX in Jacksonville, Florida; WTOF in Canton, Ohio; and the entire Jack Mortenson chain—WMUZ in Detroit, Michigan; and WBFZ in Detroit and all the Don Crawford chain of stations. It was growing almost faster than I could comprehend it.

Eventually, we would go on some 600 radio stations daily all over America, sometimes airing as much as three times a day over a single station.

THE HOLY SPIRIT

After I had been on the air for possibly two or three months, the Spirit of the Lord spoke to my heart and stated, "I want you to start teaching on the Holy Spirit."

I immediately informed the Lord that I was an evangelist and not a teacher. Still, I couldn't get away from what the Lord was speaking to my heart. I'll never forget the moment when the Lord told me, "I'm going to show you how to teach."

And He did exactly that which I have just stated, with it taking about 15 minutes, and I have followed the pattern that He gave me from then until now.

I began to teach on the Holy Spirit—the baptism with the Spirit, speaking with other tongues, the gifts of the Spirit, and the fruit of the Spirit. At that time, there was a great move going on all over the world, especially in America, regarding the baptism with the Holy Spirit—Baptists were being baptized with the Spirit; Methodists were being baptized with the Spirit; and even Catholics were being baptized with the Spirit.

I suppose I taught on the Holy Spirit for as much as two years or longer. More than likely, it was through the entirety of the radio programming, which lasted until we went on daily television.

I've had preachers ask me to tell them what the Lord gave me, and I have tried to do it in a couple of cases, but I could tell they didn't understand.

At about this particular time, crowds in the churches where we were preaching revivals grew so large that people were being turned away for lack of seating, and it was all because of the radio programming.

I preached and taught on the Holy Spirit so much that I would receive letters in the mail addressed to "Mr. Pentecost" and the post office knew where to deliver them.

Of the thousands upon thousands of letters that we've received, several stand out in my mind. You might find the following interesting.

TOLEDO, OHIO

The auditorium that contained our meeting in Toledo was not large, possibly seating only 1,000 to 1,500 people.

This particular night, it was so filled that if the fire marshal had known the size of the crowd, he probably would have tried to force several hundred to leave. At any rate, the Lord moved mightily that night.

After the meeting was over, I received a letter from a dear brother who had given his heart to Christ that evening.

He told me how his life had been one of crime. Actually, he was one of the hitmen for the mafia in that part of the world. He had started listening to the radio program and gotten under conviction. He decided to come to the service that night and responded to the altar call.

He related in his letter how that he went to the mafia chieftain and told him what had taken place in his life, and that he would no longer be in the mafia. He said, "Brother Swaggart, I didn't know what he would do. Would he kill me?"

At any rate, that mafia leader looked at him for awhile and finally stated, "You are serious about this, aren't you?"

"Yes," he said, "I've never been more serious in my life."

His letter went on to say, "I gave the man my word that I would never say anything about what had taken place during those years of doing the things that I had done—some of them awful."

He told how the man looked at him again and said, "I believe you, and if you do what you said, you'll have no fear from us."

THE MOST POPULAR PROGRAM

I remember one particular group of stations that our program was on, with the exception of one station. I kept trying to get the man responsible to air our program over that station, and he kept telling me, "Brother Swaggart, you won't go over in that part of the world." It was somewhere up in New England. Finally he relented and aired it.

A few weeks after we had gone on that particular station, this man called me and said, "I don't understand it." He explained that they had taken a poll to see what the most popular program was on that particular station, and he said, "Brother Swaggart, you came out number one." In other words, our program was not only the most popular program on that one station, but it was also the most popular on all of his stations.

He didn't understand that it was the anointing of the Holy Spirit on the programming, whether the music or the teaching, that made it what it was.

THERE IS A RIVER

It was about this time that I recorded the song, "There Is A River." I had already recorded possibly 10 or 15 albums, but this particular song came about in a very beautiful and, yet, strange way.

We happened to be home on this particular Saturday and not in a meeting somewhere, which was most unusual. I heard a knock at the front door and when I opened it to see who it was, a young boy was standing there. Actually, that young man was David Sapp, who, at that time, was only 17 years old.

He said, "Brother Swaggart, I've just written a song, and I would like for you to hear it." David lived in Dallas, Texas, and had flown over to Baton Rouge, taking a chance that I was in town. He came to bring me this song.

At any rate, my mind instantly went to the peculiarities of such a thing because most people who think they can sing *can't*.

David sat down at the piano and the difference was, the young man could sing. I mean he had a tremendous voice. He began to play the piano and sing this song:

There came a sound from heaven,
As of a rushing mighty wind,
It filled every heart with singing,
And it gave them peace within,
The prophet gave the promise,
He said the Spirit shall descend,
And from your innermost being,
A river with no end.

There is a river that flows from deep within,
There is a fountain that frees the soul from sin,

Come to these waters, there is a vast supply,
There is a river that never shall run dry.

There came a thirsty woman,
That day to Jacob's well,
Her life was ruined and wasted,
Her soul was lost as well,
She came unto the Master,
And He forgave her all her sin,
And said, If you drink of this water that I give you,
You'll never thirst again.

There is a river that flows from God above,
There is a river filled with His great love,
Come to these waters, there is a vast supply,
There is a river that never shall run dry.

As that young man began to sing, I knew the Lord had given that song to him, and it just so happened that we were leaving the next day for Nashville to record a new album.

THE RECORDING SESSION

If I remember correctly, we were in Columbia Studios, studio B. Even though there would be nine other songs on that album, "There Is A River" would be the lead song.

Now recording in those days was very different from the present. Actually, as I dictate these notes, I have just left our studio where I listened to my newest album that's just been finished. The name of it is, *There Is a Balm in Gilead*. Anyway, if mistakes are made, they can be rectified instantly by electronics. However, that was not the case then.

I remember being at the piano in the studio, and the song was going forth. I could sense the moving and the operation of the Holy Spirit. I was praying inwardly that no one would make a mistake, for if someone did, we would have to start all over again. But no mistakes were made.

There were quite a number of people in the studio when I was recording. As it was being played back for us to see if everything was alright, I looked at grown men and saw tears rolling down their faces as the Spirit of God moved on that song.

A few weeks later, we aired it over our radio program, and it stayed number one in gospel music in America for two years.

I remember one dear lady wrote, "When you started playing that song, I sensed the presence of God so mightily, and when I came to, I was on the floor as the Spirit of God had knocked me flat on my back."

HEARD IN REMOTE VILLAGES

I remember a particular preacher telling me how that he was going to have the privilege of ministering to a tribe in Africa, which, he was told, had never heard the gospel. He was eager to get there. When he was coming into the village, he heard something that he didn't expect to hear. He heard the song, "There Is a River."

They were playing it on an apparatus that was for the entire village.

When he arrived, he asked where they had gotten the recording. I don't remember the answer, but they told him how that they had given their hearts to Christ, even though they really did not understand the words as they did not speak English.

In fact, as I've already explained in this volume, the Lord has helped us to touch the world to a degree with our music. Of course, we give Him all of the praise and all of the glory.

As I've already explained, it goes back to that night when, as an 8-year-old boy, I asked the Lord to give me the talent to play the piano. He not only gave me that talent, for which we will ever thank Him, but He also gave me an understanding of music regarding what the Holy Spirit wants and desires, for which we will be ever so thankful.

If you hear our music, even though there is no name attached, you can pretty much tell if it's ours. It doesn't matter where you are in the world when you hear it. It has that certain sound.

OUR FIRST STATION

At that time we owned a 5,000 watt AM station in Baton Rouge. It was our first station, and the way it was obtained is, I think, worth telling.

It must have been about 1966 or 1967. There was no gospel radio station in Baton Rouge, and at a point in time, I felt led of the Lord to try to obtain a Christian radio station in our city. I had heard of an AM station that had gone bankrupt, so I set out to try to obtain that particular station. As previously mentioned, I knew nothing about radio in those days, much less how the Federal Communications Commission (FCC) worked, as it regards all the rules and regulations.

At any rate, I did whatever I could do to find out how to get the station, all to no avail. Finally, I was told that the station was to be auctioned off and that $80,000 was the limit that could be paid for the station. (Later, they found out that was a mistake, but it saved the ministry $40,000 or $50,000 dollars.)

The day arrived that the auction was to take place and a referee, appointed by the FCC, was present.

Some weeks before, some special guests were at our house, and we were discussing our efforts to try to get the station. All of a sudden, this young lady spoke up, and it was obvious that the Spirit of the Lord was on her. She said, "Brother Swaggart, you are going to get that station." It was just that short, and to the point.

The Spirit of God went all over me, and I knew the Lord had spoken. How it would be done, of that I had no idea, but I'd learned to trust God and watched Him do amazing things.

THE AUCTION

We had hired a lawyer out of Washington, and I found out later that he was one of the most knowledgeable lawyers concerning FCC law.

As I got ready to leave, the Lord spoke to my heart, and told me to do something that I didn't quite understand: "Go to the bank and get $100,000."

I wondered in my spirit as to why I should do this. But the Spirit of the Lord continued to impress me: "Go to the bank and get $100,000."

I did what the Lord told me to do. Actually, I got $100,000 worth of CDs. I put them in an envelope, and placed them inside my coat pocket. Little did I realize that this would ensure us getting that station.

THE AUCTION BEGINS

The referee, who was a judge from Baton Rouge, laid down the rules as to how the auction would be conducted. There was one other man bidding against me. He wanted to turn the station into a rock 'n' roll station or something of that nature and of course we would turn it into gospel if the Lord helped us to get it.

The referee said, "$80,000 is the limit that we can bid." Then he turned to the other man and asked him what he would bid for the station, and the man stated, "$80,000."

He turned to me and asked the same question, and I said the same thing. Now we had a dilemma. Both had bid $80,000, and how were we to break the tie?

The lawyers began discussing it as to what the law was in the state of Louisiana, etc. Then the Lord spoke to me, and suddenly I knew why He had told me to get the money.

I spoke up to the referee and said, "Your honor, he has bid $80,000, and I have bid $80,000, but how do we know that he has $80,000?"

He piped up and stated, "Well I don't have it here, but I can get it!"

My lawyer was punching me in the ribs, in essence telling me to shut up. I ignored him, and kept on pushing the situation. I stated, "He says he can get the money, but how do we know that he can?" And then I continued, "And if he can't get the money, what happens then?"

I wondered when they would catch on, and finally they did.

The other man spoke up and said, "Well how do we know that you have the money? You have been talking a lot, but can you produce the $80,000?"

I heard my lawyer sigh because he thought that I had talked myself into a trap. Slowly, I reached into my coat pocket and pulled out the envelope containing the $100,000 of CDs.

I said, "Here is $100,000."

You could have heard a pin drop in the room. The referee got up from his desk, walked around and stated, "I've never seen $100,000 in my life." He turned to the other man who was bidding against me, and said, "Can you match it?"

Of course he couldn't. I'll never forget what he did—he slammed shut his briefcase, stood up and said, "I should have been a preacher." Then he turned and walked out.

Less than a week later, I awakened that particular morning, turned on the radio to the frequency in question, and the song was playing, "In the Shelter of His Arms." That's how the Lord does things. When it was all over, my Washington lawyer stated, "I've been working in radio all of my life, and I have never seen anything like that."

Hallelujah what a thought!
Jesus full salvation brought
Victory, yes victory;
Let the powers of sin assail
Heaven's grace shall never fail,
Victory, yes victory.

From this one station would eventually come the SonLife Radio Network.

Oh my brother, do you know the Saviour,
Who is wondrous kind and true?
He's the Rock of our salvation!
There is honey in the Rock for you.

Have you tasted that the Lord is gracious?
Do you walk in the way that's new?
Have you drunk from the living fountain?
There's honey in the Rock for you.

Do you pray unto God the Father?
What will You have me to do?
Never fear, He will surely answer,
There's honey in the Rock for you.

Then go out through the streets and byways,
Preach the Word to the many or few;
Say to every fallen brother,
There's honey in the Rock for you.

AMAZING
GRACE

CHAPTER 12

TELEVISION

"Running a daily 30-minute program and airing programming 24 hours a day is comparable to a rowboat and an aircraft carrier. Both are ships, but that's where the similarities end."

TELEVISION

IF I THOUGHT RADIO was hard, I was to find out that television was in a world all its own. This was in the early 1970s, and a lot of the equipment that we presently have was not available then.

I remember when the Lord began to deal with me about television. To be sure, I did not acquiesce at all at the beginning, greatly suspecting that it was not going to be an easy task.

We began with a 30-minute program and then graduated to a one-hour program that was aired each week. I remember getting phone calls and letters from preachers telling me that I would destroy our television work if I went from 30 minutes to an hour. The Lord had plainly told me to go to an hour and to include the altar call. Many preachers were opposed to that as well.

Sometime later, the Holy Spirit began to move on me to air over television the Sunday afternoon services, which, in those days, were always dedicated to believers being baptized with the Holy Spirit. If you think including a regular altar call raised a firestorm, this one really did, and it was much larger!

"You must not do that," many said. But once again, the Holy Spirit greatly moved upon my heart to do this, and the results were that we saw a great harvest of souls.

I believe I can say without fear of exaggeration that it was the greatest harvest of souls that has ever been seen or witnessed. This was true for the crusades and especially by television. Literally hundreds of thousands came to a saving knowledge of Jesus Christ because of these meetings and the television services. As well, untold thousands were baptized with the Holy Spirit, of which I will have more to say shortly.

NEEDING HELP

I've always been a stickler for quality. I wanted the television programs to look right, sound right, and be right. After all, it was for the Lord, so it should be the best.

Before we went to the one-hour program, as stated, we were taping a 30-minute program. We were first making the programs in Baton Rouge, then in New Orleans, and then in Nashville. The situation in Nashville was much better because they made network programs in the same studio in which we were taping our programs.

Still, I was as green as grass and really didn't know what I was doing. But little by little we began to learn, and through it all, the Holy Spirit would give us His anointing, and that is what made the difference.

One particular session in Nashville took place, which was somewhat ironic. I was walking down the hall of that giant studio, and a man stepped out from his office and asked to see me for a few minutes. I wondered what he wanted.

He told me that in just a few days, he was to audition for a nationwide daily network program, which had not been done previously. There was one other man who was auditioning, as well, and that's who he was up against.

As it turned out, the man speaking to me was to be paired against Phil Donahue, and he said something that somewhat set me back.

He said, "Every time I walk down the hall, I stop and watch your taping." They had a big room there where whatever was being taped could be seen by those who were in the hall.

He said, "I have watched you very carefully. One moment you are laughing, and the next moment you are crying." Then he said, "How do you do that? If you will tell me how you can change like that, I think I can come out on top with that audition."

I tried my best to explain. I said, "What you're seeing is not really Jimmy Swaggart, but rather the Holy Spirit. It's the anointing of the Holy Spirit that helps me to proclaim the message that I'm trying to deliver. Sometimes, it will bring laughter, and sometimes it will bring weeping. But I have no control over that. It is all the Lord."

He didn't have the faintest idea what I was talking about, and, of course, I knew that he didn't.

He must have been very good at his trade, or they wouldn't have asked him to audition. However, Phil Donahue walked away with the audition and began a daily program that was to become a staple all over America.

TAPE THE SERVICES

As far as I know, there was no Christian organization anywhere that was taping live services at that time. It must have been about 1973 or 1974. Our first effort was in Indianapolis, Indiana. We hired one of the local television stations to tape it. They did the best they could, but this was out of their league as well.

Our next meeting was to be in Los Angeles, California. I heard of a unit in Florida that did some live taping, and I contacted them. They taped the Los Angeles crusade. They had some of the finest individuals in the world as far as talent and ability were concerned, but their equipment left something to be desired.

A week or so later, Dave Cooper, who owned that effort, walked into my office and bluntly stated, "I want to sell you my equipment and go to work for you." I stared at him, not knowing what to say. I laughed and said, "Dave, your equipment is not worth much." It was the talent that I needed, and it was the talent that I got.

Dave brought all of his people onboard, and they were some of the finest television people in the world. Incidentally, Dave Cooper still works for us. We turned out in those days, I believe, some of the finest programming in the world. At that time, only the major networks had the giant mobile units, but as far as I know, we were the first Christian organization to outfit a tractor trailer to tape the giant crusades.

It was to later change, but as far as I know, we were the first Christian organization to do such. We would tape the crusade services and then a little later, show them over our network, which by and large covered the nation, plus many other parts of the world. I will touch on that a little later.

It was the Lord who put all of this together. As previously stated, I believe that it resulted in the greatest harvest of souls that has ever been witnessed or experienced. It was amazing what the Lord did, which could be construed only as a miracle.

CALIFORNIA

One of the men who worked for our organization called me one day and stated that a particular couple wanted him to renew their wedding vows. He then told me a story that was miraculous.

The husband had left the home several years before because of alcohol. He was bound by that monster until it wrecked his marriage, wrecked his home, and wrecked his life. He went to Los Angeles and literally lived on the streets for months at a time, if not for several years.

He had learned how to get a drink of alcohol without paying for it. Whenever a ball game was being played, irrespective of what kind of game it was, the television sets in the bars would be tuned to the game. The biggest games were usually played on Sundays. He would go into the bar and wait for a crucial moment in the game to build—a touchdown or a home run—and then he would jump up and turn the television set to another channel, which would, of course, cause an uproar. But because they didn't want to miss the crucial play, almost everyone in the bar would jump up to get the channel back to where it was. And when they did, this man would sneak one of the drinks off of a table, and the people in the bar would never know who did it.

He did the same thing on this particular Sunday morning: At a crucial moment in the game, he turned the channel, which, of course, created an uproar. Only this time, when he turned the channel, he accidently turned it to the channel airing our programming.

And, at that exact moment, while the people in the bar were scrambling to get to the television set to turn the channel back, I made this statement in the message I was preaching: "Alcohol is wrecking your life, and if you don't allow Jesus Christ to come into your heart, it's going to kill you." It was just that quick and just that simple. The Holy Spirit had that channel to turn at that precise moment.

The man, if I remember correctly, never touched his drink. He walked out of the bar as Holy Spirit conviction gripped his soul, leaned up against the wall, and said, "Lord, if You will have a drunk, and I'm about as bad as they come, I'll give the rest of my life to You."

Right then and there, leaning up against a bar in Los Angeles on skid row, Jesus Christ came into his heart.

LOOK WHAT THE LORD HAS DONE

He hitchhiked home. He tried to clean himself up as best he could, not really even knowing if his wife still lived in the same place or not. It had been several years since he had been home, several years since he had seen her, and several years since he had seen the children.

When he arrived at the house, he walked slowly up the steps and knocked on the door. When his wife opened it, she almost fainted.

He stood there and said, "A few days ago, I gave my heart and life to Jesus Christ, and if you'll have me back, I want to come home."

And yes, the preacher who worked for us performed the renewal vows of their marriage. That's what the Lord is able to do, and what the Lord alone is able to do.

LOS ANGELES AGAIN

In those days, someone sent me an envelope with two pictures in it. They were both of a man, actually, the same man—one taken before he came to Christ and the other after he came to Christ. The first picture showed a man who was broken—hair matted and dirty, beard scraggly on his face, and lines of worry on his countenance, despite his youthful age.

The second picture portrayed the same young man, but now he had on a suit of clothes, his hair was neatly cut and combed, his face was neatly shaved, and he had a Bible under his arm.

The following is the story behind those two pictures.

This man was bound by drugs. Despite every effort he made, he couldn't quit. He had gone as far as he could and was now determined to take his life. He took all the money he had and bought all the dope he could buy, intending to overdose. He went to a little cheap motel, rented a room, and went through the door, not to come back through it—at least not alive.

His sister was concerned about him, sensing that something very bad was wrong. Of course, she knew of his terrible drug habit and of his efforts to try and quit, which had been to no avail.

Everywhere she looked that Sunday morning she couldn't find him, so she just started going from motel to motel on that particular strip, fearing the worst.

She came to the motel in question, asked the clerk if someone had rented a room, and then gave the description of her brother. The clerk looked at her and said, "Yes. He is here," and gave her the room number.

She was scared to death of what she was going to find. She hesitantly knocked on the door, and almost immediately it opened. But instead of seeing her brother high on drugs and out of his mind, she saw an entirely different person. He was smiling, even laughing, and of all things, he was saying, "Praise the Lord. Praise the Lord."

Then he told her his story, how he had checked in the night before intending to take his life, only something else happened.

He had turned on the television set, not really knowing or caring what was being aired. Our program came on, and the Spirit of God was in that program. The Spirit of the Lord reached out to him and sobered him up, so to speak, and set him free.

When I prayed the sinner's prayer that Sunday morning, he prayed it with me, and his world changed.

Enclosed with the two photographs that this man had sent me was a letter. In it he told me that he was now preaching the gospel of Jesus Christ.

Look what the Lord has done!

These illustrations that I have given are just a few of the many thousands that could be given as the Spirit of God moved through the television airwaves to touch hearts and lives, sometimes a world away.

Hear the blessed Saviour calling the oppressed,
"O ye heavy laden, come to Me and rest;
Come, no longer tarry, I your load will bear,
Bring Me every burden, bring Me every care."

Are you disappointed, wandering here and there,
Dragging chains of doubt and loaded down with care?
Do unholy feelings struggle in your breast?
Bring your case to Jesus, He will give you rest.

Stumbling on the mountains dark with sin and shame,
Stumbling toward the pit of hell's consuming flame,
By the powers of sin deluded and oppressed,
Hear the tender Shepherd, "Come to Me and rest."

Have you cares of business, cares of pressing debt?
Cares of social life or cares of hopes not met?
Are you by remorse or sense of guilt depressed?
Come right on to Jesus, He will give you rest.

Have you by temptation often conquered been?
Has a sense of weakness brought distress within?
Christ will sanctify you, if you'll claim His best,
In the Holy Spirit, He will give you rest.

Come unto Me, and I will give you rest,
Take My yoke upon you, hear Me and be blest;
I am meek and lowly, come and trust My might;
Come, My yoke is easy, and My burden's light.

AMAZING GRACE

TELEVISION
TRANSLATION

"We believe our commission from the Lord is the entirety of the world."

Minnie Bell Swaggart with Jimmy in 1937.

BELOW W.L. Swaggart, Jimmy, and Minnie Bell in 1936.

LEFT Congregation stands in front of First Assembly of God church in Ferriday, Louisiana.

The Swaggart family in 1943. From left, Jimmy, W.L., Minnie Bell, and Jeanette.

Sweethearts, Jimmy Swaggart and Frances Anderson.

ABOVE Jimmy starts full-time evangelist work in 1955.

LEFT Music has always been part of Jimmy's ministry. Here he is playing the accordion for a 1958 church revival.

A new generation of Swaggarts: Jimmy, Donnie, and Frances.

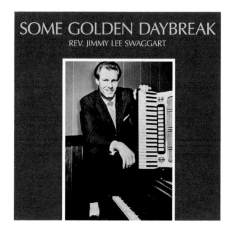

SOME GOLDEN DAYBREAK
REV. JIMMY LEE SWAGGART

Jimmy's first album, *Some Golden Daybreak* was produced in 1958, just three years after he started in full-time ministry.

RIGHT In 1969, *The Camp Meeting Hour* first aired, and Jimmy Swaggart Ministries has been on radio ever since.

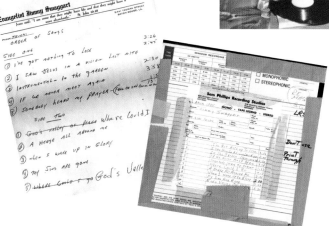

Original song lists from one of Jimmy Swaggart's earliest albums, *Nothing To Lose*, recorded in 1965 at Sam Phillips' recording studio in Memphis.

Jimmy, Donnie, and Frances Swaggart in 1966.

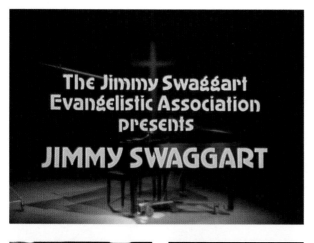

In 1973, original production of the weekly television program included taping 24 shows, each one 30 minutes in length, within a one-week period. This, added to the growing demand for evangelistic meetings, made for a brutal schedule.

RIGHT AND BELOW Musical and vocal talents were family traits for Minnie Bell, W.L., Jimmy, and cousins Mickey Gilley and Jerry Lee Lewis.

From the start of Jimmy Swaggart Ministries, Frances has played an integral role. She currently hosts her 2-hour call-in program, *Frances & Friends*, serves as the ministry's chief financial officer, and oversees a workforce of more than 300 employees.

The Evangelist started as a 4-page newsletter, written entirely by Jimmy Swaggart. Today, it is a 52-page full-color magazine with multiple contributors and ads that feature JSM products including books, music, and Bibles.

Goya Street, Baton Rouge: The first official office spaces of Jimmy Swaggart Ministries.

When churches could no longer contain the crowds, Evangelist Jimmy Swaggart traveled to nearly every major city in the United States where thousands packed out local convention complexes and sports arenas.

The Jimmy Swaggart crusades, held in the United States and around the world, made it possible for hundreds of thousands to attend and hear the gospel of Jesus Christ. Once televised, Jimmy Swaggart's music and ministry reached millions more each week. Today, the classic crusades continue to minister, airing daily on SBN, which has a potential audience reach of 2 billion people through multi-media platforms.

The ministry's call to world evangelism included crusades in Argentina, Brazil, Canada, Chile, Costa Rica, Dominican Republic, El Salvador, Guatemala, Honduras, Ivory Coast, Jamaica, Liberia, Nicaragua, Panama, Paraguay, Peru, Philippines, Russia, and South Africa.

Jimmy Swaggart Ministries world outreach efforts included the provision of food, clothing, and medical supplies to its schools and local refugee camps in places like Zaire and Zimbabwe. Without these schools, thousands of children would have gone without an education or a daily meal.

Jimmy Swaggart Ministries built or financially supported the building of churches, schools, and Bible schools in several countries including El Salvador, Guatemala, Costa Rica, Haiti, and Jamaica. The ministry built 144 schools—many with churches attached—and partially constructed 96 more for a total of 240 educational facilities worldwide.

The headquarters of Jimmy Swaggart Ministries, situated on 100 acres in historic Baton Rouge, Louisiana, is a multi-facility complex that serves as the broadcasting hub for both SonLife Radio and the SonLife Broadcasting Network. The ministry employs more than 300 people skilled in television production, commercial printing, warehouse shipping and receiving, administrations, and customer service.

1984: The Swaggarts celebrate the official dedication of Family Worship Center—the home church of Jimmy Swaggart Ministries—capable of seating up to 7,000 people in one service. From left, Donnie, Debbie, Jennifer, Frances, Jimmy, and Gabriel.

The spiritual and academic education of believers is a priority of the Swaggart family, which is why every level of Christian learning is represented on the JSM campus, from Family Christian Academy, pictured below, (preschool through grade 12) to the Jimmy Swaggart Bible College & Seminary, above, which offers numerous degree programs and online courses.

On more than one occasion, Jimmy and Frances Swaggart were invited to the White House during the Reagan and Bush administrations to discuss religious matters of national interest. In the course of their ministry, the Swaggarts were sought out by other heads of state who wanted to meet the evangelist who was drawing enormous crowds around the world with a message of morality. Others, such as Israeli Prime Minister Yitzhak Rabin, simply wanted to express his appreciation for the evangelist's unwavering support of Israel.

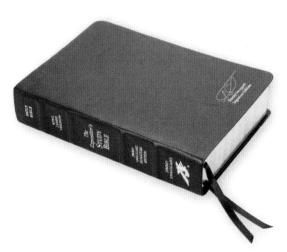

ABOVE In 2005, Jimmy Swaggart released his life's work, The Expositor's Study Bible. To date, more than three million of these Bibles have been sold and more than one million donated by viewers for pastors in Third World countries.

SonLife Broadcasting Network is the ministry-owned and operated 24-hour network that broadcasts JSM programming to 90 million homes in the U.S. and 240 million homes worldwide, as well as access through Internet and social media platforms.

Jimmy Swaggart in Jerusalem.

Close to 100,000 people to date have become media church members of Family Worship Center, made possible by the SonLife Broadcasting Network.

Donnie Swaggart grew up on the evangelistic circuit, traveling with his parents throughout the U.S., and eventually the world, helping the ministry to grow. In the 1980s, Donnie was the primary architect of the Jimmy Swaggart crusades, both at home and abroad. Now an evangelist in his own right, Donnie has more than 30 years of preaching experience including outreaches to Africa, Australia, Canada, Europe, and South America. Additionally, Donnie Swaggart co-pastors Family Worship Center and co-hosts *Frances & Friend*s. Newer projects include his creation of SBN programs *Preachers, Patriots & Providence* and *The Story Behind the Song.*

Gabriel Swaggart has been in full-time ministry since 2002. At Family Worship Center, he serves as an associate pastor and leads Crossfire Youth Ministries, including the annual International Youth Conference. On SBN, he hosts the programs *Generation of the Cross* and *Living Waters*. Gabriel's newest ministry undertaking will be presiding over Jimmy Swaggart Bible College.

Family is treasured by the Swaggarts. Jimmy and Frances are blessed with three grandchildren by Donnie and Debbie: Jennifer, Gabriel, and Matthew; two great-grandchildren by Jennifer and Cliff: Harper and Harrison; three great-grandchildren by Gabriel and Jill: Samantha, Abby, and Caroline; and three great-grandchildren by Matthew and Joanna: Ryder, Lola, and Navy.

TELEVISION TRANSLATION

IF I THOUGHT TELEVISION per se was hard, I was to learn that television translation was just as difficult, if not more so.

I can remember where I was in my prayer room when the Lord began to speak to my heart about translating the television programming into various languages in order to air the telecast around the world.

In those days, we had a one-hour program that was aired once a week (preferably on Sundays), and then we had a 30-minute program that was aired daily, Monday through Friday. While the 30-minute daily was aired in quite a few places, it was the one-hour weekly program that really touched this world.

As far as I know, we were the only Christian network at that time that was translating into other languages. And, if I remember correctly, we translated into approximately 20 different languages including: Spanish, Portuguese, French, German, Japanese, Russian, Italian, Dutch, Persian (Farsi), Swahili, Xhosa (Zulu), Arabic, Thai, Chinese (Mandarin for Taiwan), and Afrikaans.

When the services were translated into another language, the people saw me preaching, but there was actually another voice—the translator's—that was being heard. Our translators had to say exactly what I said, with the same inflections and the same warmth (or the lack thereof), to carry forth the message that was being delivered. And God used it in a magnificent way.

And, because we had excellent people translating, it was done with such expertise that most of the people thought that I was speaking the language of the country in which the program was airing.

Many times, when traveling into particular countries to conduct crusades, the people behind store counters, etc., would recognize me and start speaking to me in their language. But when I didn't answer, they were somewhat confused because they thought the voice that they heard on television was mine when it wasn't.

JIM WOOLSEY

I may be wrong, but I think the first country in which we aired the program in their language was Guatemala. We went on television over the entirety of that country.

It was there that I asked Jim to come onboard in order to get the programming on all over the world, which the Lord greatly helped him to do.

We opened our first office in Guatemala City, and, as stated, Jim saw to that particular effort. But he was little prepared for what took place there.

As soon as we put an address on the television screen, we got from 1,000 to 2,000 letters a week. Many of these people had given their hearts to Christ.

Jim kept calling here to Baton Rouge, stating that he needed more room, and he needed more help to manage the massive response. We could hardly imagine what was happening, but it was soon to be like that all over the world.

That's the reason I say that we saw the greatest harvest of souls that had ever been seen, witnessed, or experienced, for which we give the Lord all the praise and all the glory.

What we were doing, the Lord said to do it, and we did the very best we could to carry out His command. That's the reason that it was blessed. It was of the Lord and not man.

JOHANNESBURG, SOUTH AFRICA

A city called Soweto adjoins Johannesburg in South Africa. Its population is probably about 2 million. The head of law enforcement in that area told us that the only time they had a little peace was when our program came on each Sunday. Almost everybody stopped to watch it, which meant that crime pretty well ceased during that particular hour. What a mighty God we serve!

AMUSED

I was speaking at a particular time with a preacher friend, and I mentioned to him that we were about to go on television in France, with the programming translated into French, which we did. I'll never forget his answer to me. He said, "Brother Swaggart, you will not go over in France. I would strongly advise you not to try it. They are very sophisticated people, and they will not understand your Southern ways."

I asked him what he felt would be acceptable in France. He told me how his son was there, and they loved classical piano, which his son played. I asked him if anybody had been saved while listening to classical piano. He said, "No, but one or two are interested."

We went on television in France and saw such a harvest of souls that even the people from the Trinity Broadcasting Network (TBN) wrote me a letter. They told me how they had just come back from France and had seen how the people there were being saved as a result of our telecast. Paul Crouch said to me, "We'll do anything we can to help you."

Even though the French people are very sophisticated, I have learned that whatever the country and whatever its people—their nationality, color of skin, age, or educational background—the problem is always sin, and the solution is always Jesus Christ and Him crucified.

If one will stop and think, when the apostle Paul went to different areas, even to different countries, he met up with all types of cultures, but he never changed his message, simply because it should not have been changed.

Countless times Jim would meet with missionaries in certain countries. When they would ask him what he was doing there, he would tell them that he was there to get the telecast on the air. Oftentimes they would tell him, "Brother Swaggart will not go over here," and then they would give some reason.

But every single time that we went on in these countries, we very quickly had the largest audience of any program on television, whether secular or otherwise. No, the Holy Spirit does not recognize culture, or whatever. When He moves on hearts and lives, those lives can be changed, and it doesn't matter who they are or how much education they have or don't have.

DIFFERENT!

Translating into one-hour a week is altogether different from translating 24 hours a day, seven days a week, which is what we are doing now. It's much more difficult, but, of course, it can be done. Incidentally, we are currently translating only into Spanish and Portuguese, but possibly other languages will be added a little later.

The gospel of Jesus Christ is the single most important thing on the face of the earth. That's why Jesus Himself said, *"Go ye into all the world, and preach the gospel to every creature. He who believes and is baptized shall be saved; but he who believes not shall be damned"* (Mk. 16:15-16).

Jesus also said, *"And this gospel of the kingdom shall be preached in all the world for a witness unto all nations; and then shall the end come"* (Mat. 24:14).

And these verses: *"And said unto them, Thus it is written, and thus it behoved Christ to suffer, and to rise from the dead the third day: and that repentance and remission of sins should be preached in His name among all nations, beginning at Jerusalem"* (Lk. 24:46-47).

Our network, the SonLife Broadcasting Network, goes all over the world. Over a period of time, we have received emails from literally every country in the world, even from some countries where, if the people were caught sending us an email, they would be executed. Yet they love the Lord enough to risk their situation by letting us know that we're coming into their part of the world.

Let me make this statement: As long as the gospel of Jesus Christ is America's greatest export, the jackbooted heels of foreign invaders will never walk on American soil.

That's how important the gospel of Jesus Christ is.

———⫸◇⫷———

Amazing grace—how sweet the sound
That saved a wretch like me!
I once was lost, but now am found—
Was blind, but now I see.

AMAZING GRACE

THE GOSPEL PREACHED IN COMMUNIST SOVIET UNION

"When I gave the altar call, people literally ran to the front. An electrifying move of the Holy Spirit swept through that stadium as multiple thousands came to Jesus Christ."

THE GOSPEL PREACHED IN COMMUNIST SOVIET UNION

AS OUR TELEVISION PROGRAMMING began to gather larger and larger audiences in America, plus the entirety of the world, the crusades became bigger and bigger. Soon we were filling vast stadiums around the world, with some seating as many as 100,000 people. As we have stated, the gospel is the same for everyone because the need is the same, and that need is Jesus.

If I remember correctly, the first crusade we preached outside of the United States was Guatemala City in the beautiful Latin-American country of Guatemala. The stadium wasn't overly large, with it seating approximately 50,000 people.

On Sunday afternoon, which was the last service of the crusade, the clouds began to roll in, and it looked as if we were going to have some bad weather, which we did.

We covered the equipment with tarps, but to my surprise, I don't think anyone left the stadium, even though it was raining extremely hard.

Amazingly enough, the public address system continued to work even in the slashing rain. I knew, beyond a shadow of a doubt, that if the people didn't leave, I would have to keep preaching, which I did. When I gave the altar call, there was a tremendous response and, at the same time, the rain stopped.

In all the scores of crusades that we conducted all over the world, this is the only one that I can remember where we experienced a downpour of rain right in the middle of the service. As stated, it did not deter the people. They were so hungry for the Word of God that even though soaked to the skin, they remained in their seats.

TELEVISION IN RUSSIA

In 1988, the Soviet Union was locked up in monolithic communism. This meant they were atheists, and they didn't believe that there was a God. Actually, before we went on television in that great country, (I will have much more to say about this in a moment), we journeyed to that land. It was Frances, Jim Woolsey, and me. I preached a series of meetings there, beginning in Moscow.

Every city we went to, we were required to first go see the commissar of religion, which, of course, we did. The first one was in Moscow. He spoke impeccable English and was very kind and gracious. He welcomed us into the city.

The second meeting was in Novosibirsk, which is in Siberia. When we went to this particular commissar, I was expecting the same as we had found in Moscow, but it was not to be.

I walked through the door and held out my hand to shake the commissar's, but he did not reciprocate. He stood there staring at me for a few moments and finally said to both Jim and me, "You preach against us all over the world." He went on to list several examples, which were all negative, and here we were in Siberia.

Silently, I was praying, "Lord, show me what to do." The commissar's statements were becoming harsher, and the problem was, he was telling me the truth.

As he was speaking, I noticed a long line of ribbons and medals on the commissar's suit. The Russians who had served in World War II, which they called the Great Patriotic War, loved to wear on their clothing the ribbons that they had won in combat. One in particular stood out to me, and I asked him—trying to change the subject—what it represented.

He very quickly said, "It represents the Battle of Kursk."

It just so happened that I had very recently read a book on that particular battle, which was the turning point of the war against Nazi Germany. I spoke up immediately and said, "This is where you faced the great German Tiger tanks and learned how to overcome them."

He suddenly stopped and looked at me and said, "You mean you know about the Battle of Kursk?"

I said, "Yes, I know about that battle, but I want to know more, especially to be able to talk to someone who participated in that conflict." At that time, it was the greatest tank battle that had ever been fought.

For nearly an hour, the commissar talked to me about that conflict. When we got ready to leave, he put his arm around my shoulder and said, "Young man, anything you need while you're here, just let me know, and I'll get it for you."

I had shown interest in something that was very special to him. All of that was designed by the Holy Spirit in order to maneuver us out of a very difficult situation, for which I will always thank the Lord.

KGB AGENT

When we arrived in Russia as it regarded our crusades, it was before we went on television there, so while the crowds were excellent, they were not nearly as large as the television crowds were.

At any rate, just before the first service in Moscow, our translator asked me for my notes. I told him that I did not have any notes. He looked at me very strangely and said, "I'm going to have to have some notes."

I apologized to him, but I stated that I did not preach with notes and did not have any notes. I found out just a short time later that he was a KGB agent who was supplied by the Soviet Union, which is the way they did things there in those days. I asked if we could have him removed, but I was told very politely that he was there to stay. Later on, I was to find that all of it was the Lord, which turned out beautifully.

After the service in Moscow, this KGB agent said to me, "I don't understand it. You preached for over an hour without any notes. How did you do that?"

Our next meeting was in Minsk. When we stepped off the train, there was a battery of television, radio, and newspaper reporters, and they began to pepper me with questions.

One said, "Your president (President Reagan) has stated that we are an evil empire. Is that what you say?"

I stood there before that gaggle of reporters and said, "I'm in your beautiful country for one purpose, and that is to preach the gospel of Jesus Christ. I will not get involved in political questions because I'm here but for one purpose." That seemed to satisfy them, and they went away to write their own stories.

In the service that day, with the building packed to capacity, right in the middle of the message, the Spirit of God moved in a mighty way. There was a word of prophecy that came forth from me in the middle of that message that stated, "The gospel of Jesus Christ is going to go into every town, village, and city in the Soviet Union."

When I said it, it startled me to a great degree, for how could such a thing happen, considering this was the greatest atheistic nation in the world?

When I made the statement, my interpreter—the KGB agent—who was standing a little bit behind me, did not interpret it. I thought at first that he didn't hear me, and I turned and looked at him. He was weeping. Big tears were rolling down his face. At that moment, that KGB agent gave his heart and life to Jesus Christ.

A few days later when we were leaving Moscow to fly to Hungary, he wouldn't let me go. He kept telling me, "Before you came, I did not know Him. Now, I know Him." Yes, he did!

We heard a few months later that he died with cancer. The Holy Spirit orchestrated this all of the way, and today that KGB agent is in heaven.

TV-1

It was 1988. Jim Woolsey walked into my office and said, "Brother Swaggart, I believe that I can get the telecast on the air over TV-1 in Moscow."

I looked at Jim as if he had lost his mind. The Soviet Union was communistic and, thereby, atheistic. They didn't even believe there was a God. Besides that, TV-1 was the propaganda television channel out of Moscow that went through some 7,000 repeater stations, covering all 15 of the Soviet Socialist Republics. While the KGB tried to have the telecast taken off the air, due to the demands of the people, it was allowed to remain. But, TV-1? That was something else altogether.

Let me say this quickly: It was not my faith that resulted in one of the greatest moves of God in the world. It was the faith of Jim Woolsey. I want that clearly understood.

I looked at Jim that day and finally said, "Go ahead, Jim, and do what you can." But in my heart I didn't believe that he had a chance of getting the telecast on.

Jim made nearly 30 trips to Moscow and met with the television people week after week, seemingly to no avail.

On the last trip, he told them, "You people have been putting me off now for about a year. I'm asking that the telecast be put on the air over TV-1."

The meeting ended, and Jim went back to his hotel room. The television was on, and, all of a sudden, he heard it: our telecast theme song, "Sometimes Alleluia," was going out all over the 15 Soviet Republics, translated into Russian!

The telecast remained on the air for three years and reached every part of that vast land, fulfilling the prophecy that had been given about four years before, which stated that the gospel would go into every city, town, and village in the Soviet Union. Again, what a mighty God we serve! It resulted in a harvest of souls that numbered in the hundreds of thousands. In fact, had it not been for the program, there is a possibility that what freedom is experienced now in Russia would not be there.

During the height of that crisis, whenever it looked as if it were going to go back to communism, President Yeltsin gave instructions, I am told, that they should start playing the program, and play it repeatedly, to, hopefully, calm the people. That is exactly what happened. Such is the power of the gospel.

There were powerful forces there trying to take Russia back into communism. Most of us remember President Yeltsin standing on a tank, trying to calm the people.

Incidentally, I am told that while our telecast was airing in that great country, it had the largest audience of any program on television, be it secular or otherwise.

Also, I would urge each of you to get a copy of Jim's book, *Passport to the Impossible,* if you don't already have a copy. It is as if you are reading more chapters from the book of Acts.

A LETTER WITH AN OFFERING

One particular brother wrote to me during the time we were on television in Russia, first apologizing, and then telling me the reason for the apology.

On a particular Sunday morning in the church that he attended, the pastor stated that Jimmy Swaggart was lying; that we really were not on television in Russia.

This brother had been supporting our efforts, but when he heard that, he quit. At that particular time, we had taken the ministry to the edge of bankruptcy, trying to stay on the air in Russia. It was that critical, so even the loss of one supporter hurt us greatly.

At any rate, several weeks later, not feeling right about the matter, he took it to the Lord in prayer. He asked the Lord, "Is Jimmy Swaggart actually on television in Russia, or is he lying about it as our pastor said?"

The next morning he picked up the local newspaper and was browsing through it when he saw an article that had been reprinted from the prestigious Washington, D.C., newspaper, *The Washington Post*. One of their correspondents had traveled the length and the breadth of the Soviet Union in order to write an article about what was presently taking place in that vast country.

Way down in the body of the article, the dear lady who wrote it stated, "Incidentally, everywhere I went in Russia and turned on a television set, Jimmy Swaggart was on."

The brother said that as he held that newspaper in his hand, he turned cold all over. He fell on his knees and asked the Lord to forgive him. That is what he told me in his letter, plus he enclosed an offering.

As someone has long since said, "We have met the enemy, and he is us."

ANOTHER TESTIMONY

When our telecast was on the air in Russia, I received a telephone call one day. A pastor, whom I did not know, introduced himself and told me that he had just come back from Russia. He told me how that every few months he, plus another group of preachers, would journey to Moscow. They would bring in pastors from particular churches over that vast land, pay their way to get them there, and then teach them the Word of God. It was like a cram course for the time they were there.

He went on to tell me how that some of these pastors were running several thousands in their churches, yet they knew very little of the Word of God, and it was for all of the obvious reasons.

He stated that on his last trip, at a point in time, with several hundreds of preachers present, he asked them to briefly stand to their feet and tell how they had been saved.

He said, "Brother Swaggart, 90 percent of those preachers stated that they had gotten saved by watching the telecast." He went on to say, "I felt that you would want to know that."

Oh, yes, I did!

Another pastor, Tommy Barnett, with whom I was well acquainted and respected very highly, called me. Brother Barnett had helped develop a center in Los Angeles that catered to all types of people from that great city. He told me that in their center, he asked a group one day how they had given their hearts to Christ. He said, "Brother Swaggart, virtually every one of them stated that they had been saved in their particular countries (wherever it had been outside of the U.S.) through the telecast or the crusades."

Once again, how we thank the Lord.

I love to tell the story
Of unseen things above,
Of Jesus and His glory,
Of Jesus and His love.

I love to tell the story,
Because I know 'tis true;
It satisfies my longings
As nothing else can do.

I love to tell the story;
More wonderful it seems
Than all the golden fancies,
Of all our golden dreams.

I love to tell the story,
It did so much for me;
And that is just the reason
I tell it now to thee.

I love to tell the story;
'Tis pleasant to repeat
What seems, each time I tell it,
More wonderfully sweet.

I love to tell the story,
For some have never heard
The message of salvation
From God's own holy Word.

I love to tell the story;
For those who know it best
Seem hungering and thirsting
To hear it, like the rest.

And when, in scenes of glory,
I sing the new, new song,
'Twill be the old, old story
That I have loved so long.

AMAZING GRACE

THE HOLY SPIRIT

"Without the Holy Spirit,
precious little—if anything—
is going to be accomplished
for the Lord."

CHAPTER FIFTEEN

THE HOLY SPIRIT

I PERSONALLY BELIEVE THAT without the baptism with the Holy Spirit, which is always accompanied by the speaking with other tongues, not very much is going to be truly done for the Lord. If it is to be noticed, before Jesus began His public ministry, He was first baptized with the Holy Spirit (Mat. 3:16-17). Jesus was perfect in every respect and never sinned, not even one time, in word, thought, or deed. If He needed the Holy Spirit before He began His ministry, then we definitely need the same thing.

If it is to be noticed, the last word that Jesus gave to His followers was that they had to be filled with the Spirit. To be sure, the Cross of Christ has now made it possible for every believer to have the Holy Spirit, which all do. However, that of which Jesus was speaking was the baptism with the Spirit, which would come on the day of Pentecost.

Concerning this event, the Scripture says, *"And, being assembled together with them, commanded them that they should not depart from Jerusalem, but wait for the promise of the Father"* (Acts 1:4).

If it is to be noticed, He did not suggest that they go and wait for the promise of the Father, but He rather *commanded* them.

The reason?

Without the mighty baptism with the Spirit, which gives us power, as previously stated, not very much is going to be done for the Lord.

MY GRANDMOTHER

I've related elsewhere in this volume about my grandmother, so I won't take up much time here. She was the first one in our family to be baptized with the Holy Spirit. A short time later, I was filled at 8 years of age.

In 1969, we went on radio, Monday through Friday, with a little 15-minute daily program that soon expanded to some 600 stations.

After I had been on the air for about five or six months, the Lord began to deal with me about teaching on the Holy Spirit. At a given point in time, He told me to set aside a service in our crusades in the states when I would preach on the baptism with the Spirit and pray for believers to be filled. He also told me that if I would be faithful to do what He was telling me to do, over a period of time, thousands would be filled, and that even a thousand would be filled *in a single service.*

I obeyed the Lord by doing what He told me to do. I started teaching daily on the Holy Spirit—actually, on every aspect of the great Spirit of God—over *The Campmeeting Hour,* which we have already related. In fact, at that time, there was a move of the Spirit all over the world, with people from every denomination being baptized with the Spirit with the evidence of speaking with other tongues. I would like to think that our radio program had something to do with that, for which we give God all the praise and all the glory.

THE FIRST MEETING

We were in Canton, Ohio, in a meeting that was being conducted in a particular church. The Lord was moving, with good things being done.

During the week, I started announcing that on Sunday afternoon, we were going to be in a particular auditorium in the city and were going to believe God for many people to be baptized with the Holy Spirit. As stated, there was a great hunger then in the hearts and lives of believers—of all denominational persuasions—to be baptized with the Holy Spirit.

That Sunday afternoon arrived, and sure enough, the crowd was excellent. I preached on the Holy Spirit and then invited all who desired to be filled to come forward. There must have been at least 200 people who came forward to be filled, but I really did not know what to do as it regarded praying for that many people at once to receive.

All of my Christian life, we had prayed for one or two people at a time to be filled with the Spirit—and sometimes praying for them half the night. How was I to deal with hundreds at one time?

I did the best I could but, in reality, saw almost none filled with the Spirit. Afterward, to say that I was dejected would be an understatement.

I went back to the hotel room, threw myself across the bed, and informed the Lord that I wasn't going to do that anymore.

Our next meeting was in Toledo, Ohio. The Full Gospel Business Men's Fellowship chapter was having a particular convention and had invited me to speak on Saturday morning and then pray for people to be filled with the Spirit.

I agreed to come, but to be frank, I didn't know what to do.

I awakened the morning of that Saturday meeting two or three hours before daylight, I suppose.

I lay there in the bed, praying and asking the Lord to show me what to do.

I looked in my briefcase and found an audio cassette tape there by Brother Kenneth Hagin. I had not heard it. I put it in the player, and it happened to be on this very subject of the baptism with the Holy Spirit. Actually, it was on how to pray for hundreds of people at one time and see them filled in a few moments time.

While Brother Hagin and I disagreed on some points of doctrine, we definitely did not disagree as it regarded the need and necessity of the mighty baptism with the Holy Spirit.

Our dear brother went step-by-step on that tape, telling the listener how to pray for hundreds of people at one time to be filled with the Spirit and to see them filled. I know that the Lord had me to put that tape in my briefcase, and I know that He had me to find it at that particular time.

THE MEETING

As I listened to that tape, I could sense the Holy Spirit moving in my heart, telling me, "This is the way that it is to be done." I could hardly wait for that Full Gospel Business Men's Fellowship service to begin.

I sang that morning and ministered to the people and then invited all who desired to be filled to come to the front. They lined up all the way across the front and all the way down the aisles to the back wall. Once again, it must have been a couple of hundred who came to be filled.

I handled the situation exactly as the Holy Spirit had told me to, and sure enough, I believe every single person who came forward was filled that day. In other words, well over a hundred people were baptized with the Holy Spirit in just a few minutes.

IT'S BETTER

I remember one dear Nazarene lady who would come to all of our meetings in that part of the world. She desired to be filled with the Spirit, but she had not been filled up to that time.

The Lord knocked that dear soul flat of her back, and she came up speaking in other tongues. I'll never forget what she said to me: "Brother Swaggart, it's better than what you said!"

From then on, we dedicated one service in each crusade for believers to be baptized with the Holy Spirit, exactly as the Lord told me to do.

He even told me that while He would baptize thousands over a period of time, He would fill as many as a thousand in a single service—if I would believe Him.

TELEVISION

As stated elsewhere in this volume, at a given point in time, the Lord told me to air these Holy Spirit services over television, which we did. It created a phenomenal hunger in the hearts and lives of untold thousands. And while I did see many baptized with the Spirit—actually, thousands over a period of time—I had not, up to a given point, seen a thousand people baptized in a single service, which I believed the Lord had told me would happen.

MADISON SQUARE GARDEN

Madison Square Garden, at that time, was one of the largest indoor coliseums in America, if my information is correct. Our meeting there was about the third one that we had conducted in New York City, and on that Sunday afternoon, the Garden was packed to capacity.

When I asked those who desired to be filled with the Spirit to come forward, they lined up all the way across the front, down each aisle to the back wall, and even upstairs. It was the largest response I had ever had.

After the service, we had to fly to London, England, which we did.

After getting checked in at the hotel, I told Frances that I was going out to walk and pray for a little while, which I did. The hotel was right near Hyde Park.

While in prayer in that beautiful park, the Holy Spirit began to speak to my heart and said, "How many were filled with the Spirit yesterday afternoon?"

Actually, I had not even thought about it, but all of a sudden, it dawned on me. The Holy Spirit whispered again to me, "How many were filled yesterday afternoon?"

Of course, I had no way to count the people, and that was not important, but I instantly knew that it was a thousand or more. The Holy Spirit spoke to me again and said, "If you will believe Me, you will see more than 10,000 filled in a single service."

AN AFFIRMATION

After that time of prayer in Hyde Park, I wondered if the Lord had really said that to me about 10,000 being filled in a single service, or if it had just been in my mind.

It was in 2015. Every morning, before I go to the telecast, I go before the Lord for a time of prayer. As well, each day when I go home in the afternoon, I do the same thing again.

In prayer, the Lord brought back to me a situation that took place in Madison Square Garden in New York City. He renewed my mind again as it regarded that prayer session at Hyde Park in London.

Then He spoke to my heart again and stated, "What I told you that day in London was not something in your mind. I was speaking to you. I am reaffirming that which I told you that day: if you believe Me, I will baptize as many as 10,000 in a single service with the mighty Holy Spirit with the evidence of speaking with other tongues."

I remember how the presence of God filled my heart, but the questions came thick and fast. How could it be, seeing that we aren't preaching citywide crusades now?

Then, the Holy Spirit told me, "In the morning, when you get up to preach at Family Worship Center, look at those television cameras in front of you."

All of a sudden, it dawned on me. Of all people in this world, I thought, I should have known better. I had seen the Lord move over television to such an extent that untold numbers of people found Christ as their Saviour, and many were filled with the Spirit.

The Lord said, "When My Spirit moves, it goes out over those ether waves over radio and television. As My Spirit moves, thousands can be filled as a result of a single service."

At the time of this writing, we haven't yet seen that come to pass, but we most definitely will. That I believe with all of my heart. In fact, even though we've seen some great days, some great times, and some great miracles, I believe what we're going to see in the near future is going to eclipse everything that we've seen in the past. As it was said of Jesus turning the water to wine at the marriage feast of Cana: He will save the best for the last.

I wish to say it again: Without the baptism with the Holy Spirit, which is always and without exception accompanied by the speaking with other tongues, very little is going to be done for the Lord Jesus Christ.

I'll close this chapter by saying what I said at the beginning: believers being baptized with the Holy Spirit is not a suggestion; it is a command, (Acts 1:4).

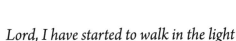

Lord, I have started to walk in the light
Shining upon me from heaven so bright,
I bade the world and its follies adieu,
I've started in Jesus, and I'm going through.

Many they are who start in the race,
But with the light they refuse to keep pace;
Others accept it because it is new;
But not very many expect to go through.

I'd rather walk with Jesus alone,
And have for a pillow, like Jacob, a stone;
Living each moment with His face in view,
Than shrink from my pathway and fail to go through.

O brother, now will you take up the Cross?
I give up the world, and count it as dross;
Sell all you have, and give to the poor,
Then go through with Jesus and those who endure.

I'm going through, yes, I'm going through;
I'll pay the price, whatever others do,
I'll take the way with the Lord's despised few,
I'm going through, Jesus, I'm going through.

AMAZING GRACE

FAMILY WORSHIP CENTER

"In reality, church is actually that which is preached and taught behind the pulpit. Everything else, one might say, is just an add-on."

FAMILY WORSHIP CENTER

FAMILY WORSHIP CENTER IS, I believe, one of the most influential churches in the entirety of the world. Actually, through television, the Internet, and social media, the services from this particular church go out all over the world each and every week. Consequently, as stated, the influence is staggering, for which we give the Lord all the praise and all the glory.

Back in the early 1980s, the ministry was growing by proverbial leaps and bounds. We were bringing in people from all over the nation to work in the ministry, and I realized we needed a church that was conducive to that which we preached and taught. Yet, Frances and I had to depend mostly on others to get it started simply because we were gone almost all of the time in crusades all over the world. As stated, through the television programming, the crowds had become astronomical.

If I remember correctly, we started in a Holiday Inn ballroom and stayed there for a period of several months. We had purchased approximately 100 acres for the new ministry headquarters and had built a structure at the back of the property, which we turned into a church for the time being. Actually, it's the same auditorium presently used for Gabriel's Crossfire Youth Ministries. But we quickly outgrew that, and I felt in my heart that we needed to erect a structure—one that would accommodate the crowds. So, I called in the architects.

THE MOVING OF THE HOLY SPIRIT

I told them that we wanted a building that would seat approximately 7,000 people, and there were other particulars as well.

Afterward, I began to get cold feet. I had started the process of building a structure that would seat 7,000 people, when the church, at that time, was only averaging about 500. Besides that, this church was going to cost many millions of dollars. (Actually, we paid for the construction of the church mostly with the sale of my albums.)

At any rate, I called the architects back in and told them to stop work on the plans; I wasn't certain as to what I should do.

Frances and I really made it a matter of prayer. We wanted the will of God and felt that we had to have the sure knowledge of His will before we proceeded further.

Then the Lord gave me a dream. I dreamed that the building was finished on the exact spot that we had told the architects it was to be built. Then, in the dream, I saw shafts of light coming down from heaven above on Family Worship Center, which didn't even really have that name then.

When I had that dream, I knew the Lord was telling me that His blessings were going to be upon this church. With peace in my heart to proceed, I told the architects, "Let's get this building constructed." That was in 1983.

1993

It was one of the morning prayer meetings. I was seeking the Lord along with others about His help as it regarded this ministry, plus Family Worship Center. The Spirit of the Lord that morning began to move on my heart, and the Lord said to me, "I will help the ministry," and to be sure, He most definitely has. Then He said, "My church (He was speaking of the church worldwide) is in pitiful condition. The whole head is sick, and the body is full of sores."

This was taken from Isaiah 1:5-6, which says: *"Why should ye be stricken anymore? Ye will revolt more and more: the whole head is sick, and the whole heart faint. From the sole of the foot even unto the head there is no soundness in it; but wounds, and bruises, and putrifying sores: they have not been closed, neither bound up, neither mollified with ointment."*

Then He said, "I am going to start a move at Family Worship Center that will girdle the globe."

As I dictate these notes, that has been some 25 years ago, but at the present time, the Lord is beginning to use Family Worship Center in that capacity. As I have previously stated, I believe that this church is one of the most influential in the world at this time. Through television programming and the Internet, we go out literally all over the entirety of the world each and every week, and I speak, of course, of the services. But in those days, now years ago, I could not see into the future. In fact, when the Lord spoke that to my heart, I knew it was Him. I had no doubt about that, but I could not see how in the world it could be brought to pass.

As many of you know, there are times that we *think* the Lord has spoken to us, and then there are times when we *know* He has spoken to us.

In fact, the Spirit of God lingered in that prayer room for quite some time, and I knew that the Lord had spoken, although I was not sure at all how He would bring this to pass.

The major theme of Family Worship Center is the Message of the Cross. It is, I believe, what the Holy Spirit is saying to the churches presently.

FAMILY WORSHIP CENTER MEDIA CHURCH

Sometime back, we felt led of the Lord to invite people from all over the world to become members of Family Worship Center. At the time of this writing, close to 100,000 people have become media church members. They believe what we teach and preach, and they want to be a part of it, despite the fact that most live far from Baton Rouge in different cities, counties, states and countries around the world.

There's only one requirement for being a part of Family Worship Center, and that is that the person be born again. There are no financial obligations, even though we strongly encourage the people to pay their tithes, and we are so grateful for those who do. As should be obvious, it costs a lot of money to bring the signal into untold millions of homes 24 hours a day, seven days a week. So, any and all help that we get is so desperately needed and so very much appreciated.

In every service, we do our very best to follow the leading and direction of the Holy Spirit, and that goes for our musicians and singers as well as each and every minister who stands behind this sacred desk to preach the Word of God. And what we preach is easily summarized in Family Worship Center's statement of faith:

- The Bible is the inspired and only infallible and authoritative Word of God (Ps. 119, Mat. 4:4; Lk. 24:27).
- There is one God, eternally existent in three persons— God the Father, God the Son, and God the Holy Spirit (I Jn. 5:7).
- We believe in the deity of our Lord Jesus Christ, in His virgin birth, in His sinless life, in His miracles, in His vicarious and atoning death, in His bodily resurrection, in His ascension to the right hand of the Father, in His personal future return to this earth in power and glory to rule a thousand years and then forever (Jn. 1:1-4; Eph. 2:13-18; Rev., Chpts. 19-20).
- We believe in the blessed hope—the rapture of the church at Christ's coming (I Thess. 4:13-18).
- We believe that the only means of being cleansed from sin is through repentance and faith in the precious shed blood of Christ (Rom. 5:1; Eph. 2:8-9, 13-18).

- We believe that regeneration by the Holy Spirit is absolutely essential for personal salvation (Jn. 3:5-8; Titus 3:5).
- We believe the redemptive work of Christ on the Cross provides healing of the human body in answer to believing prayer (Ex. 15:25-26; James 5:14-15; I Pet. 2:24).
- We believe in the sanctifying power of the Holy Spirit by whose indwelling the Christian is enabled to live a holy life (Rom. 6:3-14, 8:1-2, 11).
- We believe in the resurrection of both the saved and the lost—the one to everlasting life and the other to everlasting damnation (Rev. 20:5-6, 11-15).
- We believe and teach that everything comes through the Lord Jesus Christ. He is the source (Jn. 1:1-4; 14:6).
- We believe and teach that the Cross of Christ is the means by which all of these wonderful things are given to us (I Cor. 1:17-18; 2:2).
- Understanding that Jesus Christ is the source and the Cross is the means, the Cross of Christ must be the object of our faith (Rom. 6:1-5; Gal. 6:14; Col. 2:10-15).
- With the Cross of Christ as the object of our faith, the Holy Spirit, who works exclusively by and through the Cross, will then help us mightily. This is the manner in which He helps us to live a holy life (Rom. 8:1-11; Eph. 2:18-22).
- We believe in the baptism with the Holy Spirit according to Acts 2:4 is given to believers who ask for it (Acts 2:4; 10:44-46; 19:1-7).

It's out of obedience to Him, I believe, that we are seeing more and more people receiving salvation, healing, deliverance, and the baptism with the Holy Spirit—not only in this beautiful sanctuary at Family Worship Center, but around the entirety of the world.

Blessed assurance, Jesus is mine!
Oh what a foretaste of glory divine!
Heir of salvation, purchase of God;
Born of His Spirit, washed in His blood.

Perfect submission, perfect delight,
Visions of rapture burst on my sight;
Angels descending, bring from above
Echoes of mercy, whispers of love.

Perfect submission, all is at rest,
I in my Saviour am happy and blest;
Watching and waiting, looking above,
Filled with His goodness, lost in His love.

This is my story, this is my song,
Praising my Saviour all the day long;
This is my story, this is my song,
Praising my Saviour all the day long.

AMAZING GRACE

RADIO STATION
NETWORK

"Our love for gospel radio
knows no bounds."

RADIO STATION NETWORK

WE WENT ON DAILY radio Jan. 1, 1969. Very soon we were on some 600 stations daily, Monday through Friday. In 1972, we felt led of the Lord to go on television with a one-hour program, which would be aired once a week on Sundays, and with a 30-minute daily program, Monday through Friday. When we instituted the daily telecast, it became very difficult in trying to carry both the daily radio and the daily telecast. So, at that time, the daily radio program was canceled. That would have been about 1973.

In about 1997, the Lord began to deal with me about establishing a radio station network where we would own the stations, and we would program them 24 hours a day, seven days a week. All of this was when we had no money whatsoever. How in the world, I mused in my mind, could we carry out this that the Lord had directed us to do with no funds?

At that time, we owned a 5,000 watt AM station in Baton Rouge. At a point in time, an FM frequency (30,000 watts) came open for bidding. In other words, we, plus whoever else desired to do so, could make application to get the frequency, which would be awarded to someone by the FCC in Washington, D.C.

In those days, I little understood all the rules of radio stations and didn't realize that if you won the frequency, as we did, it really didn't mean that much. In other words, the competing applicant could turn right around and appeal again, which they did several times. The opposing side was desperately trying to prevent us from getting it. We know because Gabriel actually overheard them in a restaurant discussing how they would take the frequency from the ministry. The whole thing drug on for three or four years.

At a point in time, I put the station on the air, with the lawyers in Washington telling me that if we lost the station, we would have to give it up. Something then happened that made it even more difficult. The FCC changed the rules, I was told, which made it easier for the competing applicant to get the station. At that time, we only had two stations—the station in Baton Rouge that I am addressing now, and a 5,000 watt AM station in Bowling Green, Ohio. This was a powerful station, covering almost all of the lower part of Ohio, and even some of Michigan.

The situation in Baton Rouge was becoming more and more difficult, with the other side looking as if they would finally win in the end. I did what I always did about problems: I went to prayer.

PRAYER

I went before the Lord that afternoon and told Him our problems and asked Him to move so that we would gain the station. We had to have it, for it would be the mother station for all of the other stations we hoped to acquire. In other words, the entire network, which then did not exist, depended on us getting this station.

I told the Lord that day that I needed an answer from Him. I will not forget my statements. I said, "Lord, I've been living for You a long time, and I should not need any sign. You know my heart. This thing has dragged on so long that I need a sign from heaven that the station is going to be ours, if You would accord me that blessing."

I went on praying about other things and actually forgot about my petition. After a short period, while praying, I began to quote the words of a little chorus that we sang quite often at Family Worship Center (and still do):

We are able to go up and take the country,
And possess the land from Jordan to the sea.
Though the giants may be there our way to hinder,
Our God has given us the victory.

When I got to the last line, "Our God has given us the victory," the presence of God came all over me, and the Lord spoke to my heart and said, "You've asked for a sign, and I've just given it to you." I left that time of prayer knowing that the Lord had heard my petition, had answered my prayer, and that the station would be ours in just a few days, and it was. The other side threw in the towel, so to speak, and the station was now ours, exactly as the Lord said that it would be.

OUR FIRST STATION IN THE NETWORK

The first full power station that we purchased (besides the two that we presently owned) was in Atlanta, Texas. It was a 50,000 watt giant FM station.

The Lord had told me that when programming these stations, I was to use nothing except that which came out of Family Worship Center. In other words, I was not to sell time to other preachers, and neither was I to play music by musicians and singers other than Family Worship Center's. When I told our people what we were doing, that is, what I believed the Lord wanted us to do, I didn't have a single one, if I remember correctly, who agreed that it would work. They all looked at me, shook their heads, and said, "You'll never make it." The Lord had spoken, and, actually, He told us to do the very same thing with television, which we have carried out to the T.

Why would the Lord want that?

I cannot answer in totality, but I think the main reason was content—what He wanted us to teach and the music that we were to play. It was not to be contradicted by one preacher coming on saying, "It is red," and another coming on saying that the same thing was blue. That would leave people confused. At that particular moment, I did not know it, but the Lord was to give us a message—the Message of the Cross. I've found that this message makes a tremendous impact on the church all around the world, which I will get to a little bit later.

That first station we bought was by paying a little down and so much a month. I soon found that the transmitter was worn out.

A transmitter for a station that size costs about $80,000—money we didn't have. In fact, we didn't have $10.

It started going off the air almost every day, and we would have to send an engineer from Baton Rouge all the way to Atlanta, Texas, which was expensive.

On the morning in question, when we finished our radio program, *A Study in the Word,* David Whitelaw walked into the studio and said, "Brother Swaggart, Atlanta is off the air again."

I was very discouraged. We had no money to send an engineer there to get it back on the air, and it didn't look as if it did much good to put it back on because it would go off again in a matter of hours or less.

I got in my car and went to McDonald's to get a biscuit or something for breakfast. I got in the line of cars, and the radio station was on to our local SonLife station. All of a sudden, this song began to come over the air:

Jesus is the One. Yes, He's the only One.
Let Him have His way, until the day is done.
When He speaks you know,
The dark clouds will have to go,
Just because He loves you so.

The presence of God filled the car. I sat there weeping as tears rolled down my face. I have learned that whenever the Spirit of God moves in such a fashion, the Lord is telling us something. He definitely was telling me something that day. He was telling me that irrespective of the present problems, everything was going to be all right. Today, the ministry owns 79 radio stations because Jesus spoke, and when He did, those dark clouds had to go.

GROWTH SPURT

During a short window of time, the FCC granted the opportunity to purchase construction permits for translator (lower power) stations throughout the United States. This window of opportunity allowed the ministry to acquire more than 30 stations in a very short amount of time, which accelerated the growth of the SonLife Radio Network.

To expand the network and its programming, we needed to purchase a satellite dish that would beam the signal nationwide. The price of that dish was $50,000—money we simply did not have. During one of our radio-thons, I felt led of the Lord to go on the air and explain to the people that this is what was needed to move the radio network forward. That day, a man walked in off the street and into the studio. "Don't worry about this," the man told me. "The Lord told me that He will provide." And He did. Later that same day, a dear lady walked into our administration building and gave us a check for the entire amount.

PALM SPRINGS, CALIFORNIA

Every one of the radio stations that we ultimately acquired had their own story to tell, but one stands out. It was in Palm Springs, California.

Frances and I were out there with friends for a few days of vacation. I took Frances to the store one particular day and waited in the car until she finished with her shopping. I searched the dials on the car, looking for a gospel station, which I did find one or two, but they had very little to say. Without the Holy Spirit, not very much is going to be done for the Lord.

I sat there in the car and began to pray, asking the Lord to give us a station in Palm Springs, California. Now, Palm Springs is one of the most prestigious cities in the world. To try to get a station in Palm Springs would take a miracle of miracles. Of course, that's the way the Lord works. He is a miracle-working God.

I will be frank with you. I didn't have a whole lot of faith when I was asking the Lord for the station in that city, realizing the impossibility of such a request, at least in the natural. Nevertheless, I asked the Lord.

Then, in a matter of hours, the Lord began to move on my heart. About a year before, a new frequency had come open in Palm Springs, and it was offered to us, but the price was $1 million. We didn't have $50, much less a million. Anyway, I felt led of the Lord to call the man who owned this new frequency and see if it was still for sale.

He told me, "Brother Swaggart, I sold the station yesterday."

His words came like a blow to my head. I thought for a moment and said, "Well, if he falls down, and they're unable to come up with the funds, would you give me a call, or better yet, I'll call you."

I knew the Lord had told me to call the brother, but I was somewhat confused that the station had already sold.

At any rate, the next day I placed a call to the man and asked him about the situation.

He said, "Brother Swaggart, it's strange. The man who agreed to buy the station yesterday has just told me that he cannot afford to go through with the deal."

I asked him, "Can we buy the station at the same price?"

His answer was immediate: "Yes, you can."

ANOTHER MIRACLE

We now had the promise of a radio station for Palm Springs, but we still had no money to buy it, and he wanted over half of the amount in cash. Once again, I went before the Lord in prayer, and the Lord told me exactly what to do.

We were going to have a fund-raising effort the next morning, which we did every month. However, the amount of money that we would take in would be $30,000 or $40,000. The Lord told me to tell the people what we were doing and that we had the opportunity to get this station, but we needed $500,000.

That is exactly what I did, and we raised over $500,000. In a matter of hours, the station was ours, with the Lord having performed a miracle. God still answers prayer!

We still owed, once again if I remember correctly, $300,000 on the station. I will ever have to thank Roy and Beulah Chacon, for they paid off the station, and there is nothing owed on it at this present time. The radio network has performed and is performing a tremendous work for the Lord, about which we will say more just a little later.

Incidentally, the type of programming that the Lord told me to carry out has worked beautifully because that's what the Lord said to do. Everything that goes out over our 79 radio stations comes from Family Worship Center. We think it's some of the finest preaching and teaching in the world, plus some of the finest music in the world that glorifies the Lord Jesus Christ and proclaims the Word without confusion.

I hear the Saviour say,
"Your strength indeed is small,
"Child of weakness, watch and pray,
"Find in Me your all in all."

Lord, now indeed I find
Your power and Yours alone
Can change the leper's spots
And melt the heart of stone.

For nothing good have I
Whereby Your grace to claim—
I'll wash my garments white
In the blood of Calvary's Lamb.

And when before the throne
I stand in Him complete,
"Jesus died my soul to save,"
My lips shall still repeat.

Jesus paid it all,
All to Him I owe;
Sin had left a crimson stain,
He washed it white as snow.

AMAZING GRACE

CHAPTER 18

REVELATION OF THE CROSS

"I believe what is happening now as it regards this ministry and the Message of the Cross is what the Holy Spirit is saying to the churches."

REVELATION OF THE CROSS

IN 1988, AT A VERY crucial time in the history of this ministry, the Lord gave me a promise that was to be one of the greatest ever.

It was a Monday, and Frances and I had stayed home from the office that day. I would spend the entire day in prayer and study of the Word.

Our house, along with Donnie's, sits on some 20 acres of land outside the city limits of Baton Rouge. I had gone to the back of the property, which affords privacy, in order to seek the Lord.

Few times in my life, if ever, have I experienced an attack by Satan as I did that morning. I will not go into any detail, but it was so bad that I even told the Lord, "You said that You would not put anything on us harder than we could bear, and that with every temptation You would make a way of escape."

I then told Him, "Lord, I dare not speak out of turn, but I think You are allowing Satan too much latitude. No human being can stand this." It was like a hundred pounds were on my shoulders, crushing me down to the ground.

Then, all of a sudden, it happened.

Instantly and immediately, the Spirit of God came all over me, and the Lord spoke to my heart and said, "I'm going to show you some things about the Holy Spirit that you do not now know."

I thought for a few moments, realizing that the Holy Spirit is God, and there are all types of things about Him that I do not know. Yet, I somehow knew that the Lord was speaking of the problem at hand, and that's what He was addressing.

I don't think I've ever felt like that in my life. It was as if I were walking on clouds. It was as if I didn't have a problem in the world. I remember that about that time, Frances called to me and said that I had a phone call.

It was a Baptist pastor who pastored one of the largest Baptist churches in America. He was gracious and kind to call. I've often wondered what the man thought of me, for when I answered the phone, I shouted about as loud as I could: "Hallelujah!"

I could tell that on the other end of the line, the dear brother was a little bit nonplussed, but, of course, he had no idea what had just happened to me. We spent a little time in conversation, with me attempting to tell him what the Lord had just done.

AN ANSWER

I knew what the Lord had told me: He would show me things about the Holy Spirit that I did not then know.

In the 1980s, in our crusades all over the world, along with television, I had seen the Spirit of God work in such powerful ways as to bring in possibly the greatest harvest of souls that the world had ever seen. In all of this, I saw the Lord do great and mighty things by the power of the Holy Spirit. I depended on Him to help me preach, to help me minister, to address the people, and to do exactly what the Lord wanted. In fact, I thought I had quite a bit of knowledge about the Holy Spirit, and, in essence, I did. What the Lord would show me, however, would be far beyond that which I presently knew.

Years passed, and at a given point in time, I asked the Lord why it was taking so long. I had not seen anything that I could label as the Lord speaking to me and showing me something about the Spirit of God.

One particular night in prayer meeting, the Lord, in a sense, answered my prayer. He said, "You have asked Me why it's taking so long."

He then gave me a passage from the Word of God that was strange, but I knew it was from the Lord, and I knew it was about this very question concerning the Holy Spirit. He said, *"Precept must be upon precept, precept upon precept; line upon line, line upon line; here a little, and there a little"* (Isa. 28:10). That was the answer the Lord gave me as it regarded my inquiry.

But what did it mean?

To be frank, I knew the Lord had given me this, of that I had no doubt. However, I did not know what it meant. Now I do.

The Lord was telling me the following: He was saying to me that everything had to be exactly as it ought to be before

He could give me that which He had promised. In other words, all the doctrine must be correct. As I look back now, He was, in effect, telling me that He would give me the information I needed, which would be the Message of the Cross, of which I had no knowledge whatsoever at that time. That was in about 1992; however, it would be 1997 before the Lord would do what He promised.

THE REVELATION OF THE CROSS

The Lord gave me this great word in three stages. There was no warning whatsoever when the first stage came, but it took place in 1997.

At any rate, I had gone to the office early, as I always did, even before daylight. I was writing the commentary on the epistle of Paul the Apostle to the Romans—specifically on the great sixth chapter of that book.

I picked up a book by a Greek scholar who had outlined the sixth chapter of Romans. Strangely enough, I had read this material previously, but it did not seem to register. That morning, in this great Message of the Cross, the Lord first of all showed me what the sin nature is.

I had never heard a message on the sin nature in my life. I had seen the term a time or two in the hundreds and hundreds of books I had read, but with no explanation given. And yet, this is one of the single most important doctrines in the entirety of the Word of God. That morning the Lord showed me exactly what the sin nature is, how it works, how it can be addressed, and how it can cause great problems for the child of God.

When a person has done everything he knows to do not to fail, but fails anyway, it leaves a void in his heart and questions with no answers: Why? How? When?

I remember walking back and forth across the floor in my office, with tears streaming down my face, as the Holy Spirit showed me the exact cause of failure. To be sure, it was a tremendous blessing to find out the reason.

THE CROSS

A few days later in one of the morning prayer meetings, all of a sudden, the Lord greatly moved upon my heart and gave me the solution to the sin nature. While He had told me much about it some days before, He did not really give me the solution to the problem. On this day, He did.

In prayer the Lord gave me a simple word, but, oh, so profound.

He said:

"The answer for which you seek is found in the Cross.

"The solution for which you seek is found in the Cross.

"The answer for which you seek is found *only* in the Cross."

He took me to the great sixth chapter of Romans—the very chapter I had been studying when the Holy Spirit opened up to me the meaning of the sin nature. Incidentally, I found out later that the sin nature was the very first thing that the Holy Spirit showed the apostle Paul. Then, exactly as He had done with me, the Lord gave the apostle the solution to the problem, which was and is the Cross of Christ. What confuses people is that the Message of the Cross, as the Lord gave to the apostle Paul, has to do far more with sanctification.

In other words, it deals more so with *how* we live for God on a daily basis—how we grow in grace and the knowledge of the Lord, and how we have victory over the world, the flesh, and the Devil.

THE HOLY SPIRIT

As the Lord gave this great word to me, as simple as it was, I instantly saw that the solution to man's dilemma was and is the Cross of Christ—that's where the victory was won. That's where Jesus met the demands of the broken law and defeated Satan and all of his minions of darkness. Yet, there was something about it that I didn't understand.

As the Lord gave me this word, He never mentioned the Holy Spirit. I knew that the Holy Spirit played a part in this, and I was to find out later that it is a major part. Yet, the Spirit of the Lord had said to me, "The answer for which you seek is found only in the Cross."

So, how did the Holy Spirit function in all of this?

As simple as it was, I knew that the Lord had given me something great, something powerful, and something that I later found out to be one of the greatest moves of God in the world. I realize that's quite a statement, but I believe it to be true.

No, it was not a revelation per se, having already been given to the apostle Paul, with most of his 14 epistles dealing with this very subject. While I continued to rejoice in this great word the Lord had given me concerning the Cross, this question continued to loom large in my thinking: How did the Holy Spirit play into all of this?

Then it happened.

THE LORD KEPT HIS PROMISE

We had just begun trying to teach this great word that the Lord had given us over our three radio stations. This particular morning was to be a red-letter day.

Loren Larson was with me that day, and the program was almost over.

It must have been about five minutes before the program ended, and I made a statement that seemed to come from nowhere.

I said, "The Holy Spirit works exclusively within the Cross of Christ and will not work outside of those parameters."

As soon as I uttered the words, I wondered where they came from. I had not read it, and I had not heard anybody say anything of that nature. I sat there for a moment in silence, stunned.

Loren spoke up and said, "Can you give me Scripture for that?"

How could I give him Scripture when I had never heard the statement in all of my life except a few moments before? I looked down at my Bible. It was open to Romans 8:2, which

I read aloud: *"For the law of the Spirit of life in Christ Jesus has made me free from the law of sin and death."*

There was the answer right in front of my eyes. The Lord was telling me how the Holy Spirit works. He works entirely through the Cross, by the Cross, and of the Cross. In fact, the Cross gave Him—and gives Him—the legal means to do all that He does. Jesus paid the price, but that opened the door for the Holy Spirit to do all kinds of great things.

Before the Cross, the Spirit of God could come into the hearts and lives of a few prophets, and that was about it. Whenever He finished His task, He would leave.

Actually, when believers died before the Cross, their souls and spirits did not go to heaven, but rather down into paradise where they were actually captives of Satan. The reason was that the blood of bulls and goats could not take away sins, so the sin debt remained, and it did remain until the Cross became a fact.

Now, the moment a person is born again, the Spirit of God can come into his heart and life, and does come into his heart and life. As well, since the Cross, when a believer dies, his soul and his spirit instantly goes to be with the Lord Jesus Christ, and is no longer a captive of Satan.

When the radio program ended, I got up from the little table where we were sitting to walk out when, all of a sudden, the Spirit of God came over me again, and the Lord spoke to my heart.

He said, "Do you remember back in 1988 when I told you that I would show you things about the Holy Spirit you did not then know?"

Of course, I remembered it. Hardly a day passed that it was not on my mind.

Then He said, "I have just kept My promise to you. I have shown you how the Holy Spirit works in the heart and life of the believer, and how the Cross of Christ gives Him the legal means to do all that He does."

ONE OF THE GREATEST TRUTHS

I personally feel that the word regarding how the Holy Spirit works is one of the greatest truths that the church will ever learn: It is through the Cross of Christ, which opens the door for the Spirit of God to do great things (Rom. 6:1-12; 8:1-11; I Cor. 1:17, 18; 2:2; Gal. 6:14; Col. 2:10-15).

Sadly, most believers do not know how the Holy Spirit works. If you ask them how it is done, most will look at you with a blank stare, not really understanding the question, much less the answer. Unfortunately, the modern church has relegated the Cross to our salvation experience only. "Jesus died for me" is, no doubt, the greatest statement that one could ever hear or speak, but that's as far as most Christians go.

As it regards the Cross of Christ, most Christians have absolutely no idea whatsoever the part the Cross plays in our everyday sanctification experience, in other words, how we live for God on a daily basis. They've never heard that and do not really know what you're talking about, even if they do hear it. Consequently, most Christians live in a state of spiritual defeat because they do not understand the part the Cross of

Christ plays. The Cross is what gives the Holy Spirit latitude to work within our lives.

WHAT THE CHURCH NEEDS

When the Lord began to open up to me the Message of the Cross back in 1997, it was like a dream come true. The freedom that this great truth brought to me was unexcelled. And yet, it's not something new but that which was given to the Apostle Paul, which he gave to us in his 14 epistles.

However, after a little bit, negative thoughts began to come into my mind about the necessity of the message. The Devil said to me that while some few may need this message, virtually the entirety of the church is doing pretty well. Looking back, it is so easy to recognize the Evil One, but at the time, dressed as an angel of light, he seemed to be plausible. I did not reveal to anyone what I was feeling in my spirit, but the Lord was very soon to address it.

Donnie was preaching. It was Sunday night at Family Worship Center. He wasn't preaching about Moses and the deliverance of the children of Israel from Egypt, but in the course of his message, he made the statement uttered by Moses to Pharaoh: *"Let My people go."*

When he said that word, *"Let My people go,"* the Spirit of God came all over me. I began to weep, actually sob, and the Lord spoke to my heart, and what He told me was not very pleasant to hear.

"My people," the Lord said, "are in the same condition presently as the children of Israel were in Egyptian bondage."

To be sure, that's a powerful statement. To think that the modern church is in the same shape as Israel of old, respecting Egyptian bondage, is beyond our comprehension. In other words, it's about as bad as it could ever be.

The Devil had almost made me believe that while the Cross was definitely necessary, still, the situation was not so desperate among God's people. However, that night, the Holy Spirit let me know that the church world is in the same condition, spiritually speaking, as Israel of old as it regards her terrible condition of so long, long ago. In other words, they were slaves to an evil taskmaster, and the Lord demanded, *"Let My people go."*

For a few minutes that night, I saw the entirety of the church world. I saw the bondage, and I saw untold millions who are being held captive by Satan in one way or the other, and I'm speaking of God's people.

In other words, as the situation was dire in Egypt at that time, at least as it regarded the people of God, likewise, it is dire at this time. In fact, the situation is far worse than even I know. The only answer is the Cross of Christ. There is no other. The church desperately needs a great rain of the Spirit.

———◇———

Sweet are the promises, kind is the word;
Dearer far than any message man ever heard;
Pure was the mind of Christ Sinless, I see;
He the great example is, and pattern for me.

Sweet is the tender love Jesus has shown,
Sweeter far than any love that mortals have known;
Kind to the erring one, Faithful is He;
He the great example is, and pattern for me.

List' to His loving words, "Come unto Me!"
Weary heavy-laden, there is sweet rest for thee;
Trust in His promises, faithful and sure;
Lean upon the Saviour, and your soul is secure.

AMAZING GRACE

HOW THE HOLY SPIRIT WORKS

"The Holy Spirit is about to do a thing that is going to make demons tremble."

HOW THE HOLY SPIRIT WORKS

IN THE PREVIOUS CHAPTER, we did address this subject to a limited degree. However, it is so vast that even what we will say presently will little give the major points of this tremendous doctrine.

Most Christians, even most Pentecostals, have not the slightest idea of how the Holy Spirit works. So, when we make the statement, "How the Holy Spirit works," what do we mean?

We are speaking of that which gives Him the latitude for all that He does. I am not speaking of the things done—speaking in tongues, gifts of the Spirit, etc.—but rather what it is that makes it possible for the Holy Spirit to do all of these things.

Pure and simple, it is the Cross of Christ (I Cor. 1:17, 18, 23; 2:2; Gal. 6:14; Col. 2:10-15).

As said in the previous chapter, most Christians relegate the Cross of Christ to the initial salvation experience, which is certainly correct, but regrettably they stop there and do not go all the way.

It should first be understood that in all of the apostle Paul's writings—and we are speaking of his 14 epistles—he deals with the Cross of Christ after our sanctification experience, but he only devotes a small portion to the Cross of Christ relative to justification.

Of course, all of it is of vast significance, but the Holy Spirit wanted us to understand that living for God on a daily basis is where the problem is.

HOW TO LIVE FOR GOD

In teaching one Wednesday night at Family Worship Center, I made the statement, "The modern Christian simply does not know how to live for God." As soon as I said those words, it was as if a gasp went up from that congregation. I am certain that if such was said to just about any Pentecostal congregation in the world, the reaction would be the same.

"What do you mean that I don't know how to live for God?" would be the answer that most would give. But the truth is, they don't know. Consequently—and we have all followed in this vein—we fail and fail and keep failing, despite everything we can do to try to address the problem, whatever the problem is.

Listen again to Paul: *"Christ sent me not to baptize, but to preach the gospel: not with wisdom of words, lest the Cross of Christ should be made of none effect"* (I Cor. 1:17).

The great apostle was not denigrating water baptism. No, he was simply stating that the emphasis must always be the Cross of Christ and not water baptism or the Lord's Supper, as important as those things might well be. It is the Cross that must ever be the object of our faith, and that is critical.

THE OBJECT OF OUR FAITH

The object of our faith is where the rubber meets the road, so to speak.

The believer should ever look to the Cross of Christ for whatever is needed. In fact, for every problem that man has—and I don't care what it might be, all the way from A to Z—the answer is in the Cross of Christ. This means that our faith must be in Christ and what He did for us at the Cross *and* maintained in Christ and what He did for us at the Cross (Gal. 6:14; Rom. 8:1-11).

While there are volumes that could be said regarding this most important subject, still, we have given you at least the rudiments of this tremendous subject. If you will learn what little we have here stated, then many other things about which you have questions will begin to fall into place.

Rescue the perishing, care for the dying,
Snatch them in pity from sin and the grave;
Weep over the erring one, lift up the fallen,
Tell them of Jesus the mighty to save.

Though they are slighting Him, still He is waiting,
Waiting the penitent child to receive;
Plead with them earnestly, plead with them gently,
He will forgive if they only believe.

Down in the human heart, crushed by the tempter,
Feelings lie buried that grace can restore;
Touched by a loving heart, wakened by kindness,
Chords that are broken will vibrate once more.

Rescue the perishing, duty demands it;
Strength for your labor the Lord will provide;
Back to the narrow way patiently win them;
Tell the poor wanderer a Saviour has died.

Rescue the perishing, care for the dying;
Jesus is merciful, Jesus will save.

AMAZING GRACE

THE EXPOSITOR'S
STUDY BIBLE

"There's nothing in the world more important than the Word of God."

THE EXPOSITOR'S STUDY BIBLE

I HAVE ALWAYS LOVED the Word of God.

As mentioned elsewhere in this volume, the Lord saved me and filled me with His Holy Spirit at 8 years old, and afterward, I devoured the Word of God. Going back and thinking about it in my mind's eye, I can still see it today.

The Scriptures were so interesting; I read them by the hour. I had a little Bible that probably cost $4 or $5, if that much. It had a zipper around it and made me very proud.

My little Bible didn't have headings or any of the other aids that make today's Bibles so easily read. I remember reading it, though, and studying it by the hour. Even though I was just a child, I would study particular passages of Scripture and meditate on them.

In all honesty, I didn't really know what meditation was, but subconsciously I gave serious thought to each passage, asking the Lord to explain it, and the Holy Spirit would open up God's Word.

Satan subsequently fought hard to destroy me, and he would have succeeded if it weren't for this foundation. My mother, dad, and I would discuss Scriptures for hours. What a blessed time that was. I can still see the living room of our little frame house.

I would sit with my mother, dad, and my sister, Jeanette, who was six years younger. We would often talk back and forth. My daddy would say, "Jimmy, what does this Scripture mean?"

I would explain it to him as best I could, and he would sit there and think about it. I don't know if my perceptions were all that deep, but he would act as if they were the greatest things he had ever heard.

My mother would say, "Oh that is wonderful." And then my dad would praise me, and I would grow by inches. It inspired me with greater delight and a desire for studying the Word further.

Beyond that, I would go out behind the house to a little log I used for an altar. I would pray there for hours on end. Many times I would put my little black Bible there and study it on my knees.

Mother and Dad encouraged me and strengthened me in every way possible. They were simple people and uneducated. They had been raised during the Depression and had no opportunity for a formal education at the college level. There were many things in the world they didn't know and many with which they were unacquainted.

I thank God I was not born into a rich mansion with all the emphasis on material things. I thank God that I wasn't born to parents who would not come to know Jesus Christ. Even though they had little education and our home was humble, we had the things that counted most: we knew God.

My parents taught me the Word of God. They instilled it in me; poured it into me; and helped me with it. They guided my life, and created a hunger in my heart that burns to this day.

A STUDY BIBLE

Sometime in the 1980s, the Holy Spirit planted it in my mind that I should compile a study Bible. I immediately dismissed it, thinking that I was overly unqualified for such a task, and of that I was correct. Then again, who can be qualified to do such a thing?

During the early 1990s, the inclination increased in that capacity. I started looking at other study Bibles but did not too much like what I saw as far as the layout was concerned. In most of the study Bibles that I had, the notes were at the bottom of the page, the side of the page, or sometimes in the back of the book. At any rate, at times it was difficult to find the notes, which I always enjoyed because it opened up the Scriptures somewhat.

Then, one particular day while writing one of the commentaries, I proceeded to dissect a Scripture, and the Holy Spirit spoke to my heart and said, "That's the way that I want you to do the study Bible."

In other words, the explanation of the Scripture would be placed in the body of the text, which is the King James Version, or at least right below it. I often tell people that the Holy Spirit told me to compile the notes for The Expositor's Study Bible. He told me how to do it, and then He helped me to do it. I did the New Testament first. I want to relate to you that which happened the moment I began this task.

I would be hard pressed to tell you how I felt. I actually believe that I sensed and felt the Shekinah glory of God. In a sense, it was the most fearful thing that I had ever experienced. I realized, at least for a few moments, what I was doing and that people would guide their lives by what was said regarding the notes in this Bible. For a few moments, I thought, "I can't do this," but then, the sweet presence of the Lord came over me, and I sensed in my spirit that I was doing what God wanted done.

THE PRESENCE OF THE LORD

When I was editing the notes, at times the Spirit of God would come over me to such an extent that I would tell Frances, "People are going to be blessed as it regards this particular Bible."

I was exactly right. They were.

THE LAWYER

Let me give you an example: It was a Wednesday night at Family Worship Center. I had just finished teaching, and the service was breaking up. A man walked up to the platform, introduced himself, and said, "Brother Swaggart, first of all, I owe you an apology."

He then went on to tell me that he was a lawyer and specialized most of all in divorce cases, in which there is always tremendous difficulties.

"I didn't like you at all," he said, "but someone gave me an Expositor's Study Bible, and, being a divorce lawyer, I was reading one particular day in the great book of Hosea." (He had been reading Chapter 3 of that book and came to verse 2.)

He said, "Brother Swaggart, when I read your notes, my mind totally changed as it regarded you, and I want to tell you what a blessing that it's been to me."

Let me quote what he had read: *"So I bought her to me for fifteen pieces of silver, and for an homer of barley, and an half homer of barley"* (Hos. 3:2).

The following are the notes that are in The Expositor's Study Bible regarding that one verse:

The redemption price of a slave was thirty pieces of silver (Ex. 21:32) and so much barley. Fifteen pieces of silver and so little barley marked the worthlessness of this slave. No one can fully understand the pain and suffering evidenced in the words, 'So I bought her to me for fifteen pieces of silver.' Gomer was now used up, therefore, wanted and desired by no one!

One can only guess at the hurt that filled Hosea's heart as he stood before Gomer. She was no doubt dressed in rags and had been reduced by abuse to less than a slave. She must have reasoned, 'How could he love me after all this?'

He could do so because about 800 years later, one would hang on a Cross, who had also been sold for thirty pieces of silver—the price of a slave. That one took her place of suffering that she might take His place of glory. And thus it is with us all!

When our dear brother read these words, he sensed the presence of God, and I believe most who read it also sense the same thing.

WORLDWIDE

I personally believe that the Holy Spirit has chosen The Expositor's Study Bible as the Bible for the 21st century. Now, let me make it clear that any Bible that is truly the Word of God is just as valuable as any other Bible. Something, however, that will help one to understand the Bible to a greater degree—and that is the reason for The Expositor's Study Bible—is valuable indeed.

The Expositor's Study Bible has been translated into Spanish, Russian, Portuguese, and Chinese. To date, more than 1.7 million of these Bibles have been placed into the hands of pastors and Christian workers in Third World countries, and this was not something born out of a committee meeting, etc.

The following is the way it happened: We were offering The Expositor's Study Bible over television. All of a sudden, a slip was placed before me that concerned one of the men of our church, Mike McMullen. He was purchasing a number of the Bibles to give out in Mexico, where he would be going shortly. As I read that note, the Spirit of the Lord moved upon me, and the Lord spoke to my heart and stated, "I want you to place The Expositor's Study Bible into the hands of every Third World pastor in the world." It was just that short, but I knew beyond the shadow of a doubt that it was the Lord.

As many of you know, The Expositor's Study Bible is almost like a mini Bible college, and it actually takes the place of scores of books that one could read about various doctrines of the Word of God.

Most Third World pastors don't have access to a Bible college, or any books for that matter regarding the Word of God. Some of them don't even have a Bible. We have given The Expositor's Study Bible to some who only had a page or two from a New Testament. We've placed some into the hands of those who pastor churches but had no Bible whatsoever. They would have to walk several miles to see a Bible, get a Scripture, and then walk back and try to preach it on a Sunday morning or whenever.

The Expositor's Study Bible gives understanding of the Word of God, we believe, as nothing else of its size and content.

LOOKING BACK

While the Lord began to move on my heart years before as it regarded The Expositor's Study Bible, still, He did not have me develop it until the Message of the Cross was a reality.

Looking back, it is easy to understand why. Had the Bible been developed before the understanding of the Message of the Cross, it would have been incomplete. Because of the understanding of the Message of the Cross, I personally believe that this Bible is the most complete Bible in the world today. Incidentally, it is King James Version.

I believe with all of my heart that the Holy Spirit has labeled it as the Bible for the 21ST century. To be sure, we give the Lord all the praise and all the glory for whatever good that this Bible brings about, and it can only be good that is brought about.

I want to thank the people all over America and around the world who help us with the distribution of these Bibles. At the time of this writing, we are shipping out about 35,000 a month. What we do, we must do quickly because there isn't much time left.

The wonderful thing about this is that we are getting calls from countries all over the world, irrespective of the denomination, asking for these Bibles. I am Pentecostal, so we deal with the Holy Spirit as we believe the Bible teaches it, which is contrary to some thinking as it regards church denominations that are not Pentecostal. Nevertheless, they are asking for these Bibles, and to be sure, we do not discriminate.

Irrespective, whether it's Catholic or Protestant, if they want Bibles and we are able to supply them, we most definitely ship them.

Every true believer loves the Word of God, and that means if you don't have an Expositor's Study Bible, you should avail yourself of the opportunity to secure one for yourself. Irrespective of how many other Bibles you might have, I personally guarantee that The Expositor's Study Bible will add to your knowledge of the Word of God. Anything that will do that, as we've already stated, is valuable indeed.

I have found His grace is all complete,
He supplies every need;
While I sit and learn at Jesus' feet,
I am free, yes, free indeed.

I have found the pleasure I once craved,
It is joy and peace within;
What a wondrous blessing! I am saved
From the awful gulf of sin.

I have found that hope so bright and clear,
Living in the realm of grace;
Oh, the Saviour's presence is so near,
I can see His smiling face.

I have found the joy no tongue can tell,
How its waves of glory roll!
It is like a great o'erflowing well,
Springing up within my soul.

It is joy unspeakable and full of glory,
Full of glory, full of glory;
It is joy unspeakable and full of glory,
Oh, the half has never yet been told.

AMAZING GRACE

CHAPTER 21

THE SONLIFE
TELEVISION NETWORK

"To my knowledge, such has never been done in the history of Christian broadcasting. It can be described only as a miracle."

THE SONLIFE TELEVISION NETWORK

AS FAR AS I KNOW, having begun in television in 1972, I have been on this medium preaching the gospel longer than anyone else in the world. How we give the Lord the praise and the glory for that.

However, up until 2010, all of our programming was a one-hour per week special, and a 30-minute daily, Monday through Friday. During those times, all the way back to 1972, some have asked me why we did not start a network. We didn't do it because the Lord did not tell me to do such, at least up until 2010.

Every morning that I come to the studio, I spend time with the Lord in prayer for the day's activities. When I go home in the late afternoon, I do the same thing again, on a daily basis. Actually, I do not remember the month in 2010 concerning that which I will relate to you, but I do know the year is correct.

As I went to prayer that afternoon, I sensed an unusually heavy moving and operation of the Holy Spirit. Then the Lord began to speak to my heart. He said, "Satan tried to close the door to this ministry in the 1990s, but I kept it open about 10 percent, at least compared to what it had once been."

That was exactly correct.

Then the Lord said, "I am about to open that door *wide*."

It was one of those times that I knew the Lord was speaking. Exactly what He meant by that, at the time I did not understand, but I knew what He said.

The next afternoon when I went to prayer, once again I sensed the moving of the Holy Spirit. The Lord spoke to me again, saying, "You misunderstood Me yesterday. You thought when I said that I was going to open the door wide that I was speaking only of the placement of the programming."

I had thought that, and for the reason that we had had great difficulty getting on any of the so-called Christian networks. Most of the time, with the exception of one or two, they not only rejected us, but they insulted us as well.

At any rate, the Lord said, "I was speaking of the placement of the programming, but I was also speaking of everything for which you have sought My face these last years."

Once again, I knew this was the Lord.

EXACTLY WHAT DID HE MEAN?

The first thought that came to my mind was the wonderful privilege that I had of Him hearing that for which I had sought His face. Of course, I know the Lord hears us when we pray. He notes every sparrow's fall and numbers the very hairs of our heads, so Him noting that for which we seek His face is minor compared to the other. Still, it thrilled me to know that He had heard my petition. I instantly began to think of the many things for which I had sought His face, and ardently so.

Television is what God had called me to do, and we had stayed on the air, despite tremendously adverse circumstances, because I knew the Lord had called me for that purpose, and I must not be disobedient to the heavenly vision. As well, there were the finances, and above all, the anointing of the Holy Spirit upon our efforts. I knew this was something that had to be, and I continue to speak of the anointing of the Holy Spirit, that is, if we were to carry out what I believe God has called us to do, which is to finish our part of world evangelism.

A few days later, several of us were seated in the boardroom at the ministry with discussion taking place about television. Actually, at that time, I had not related this to anyone except Frances. In other words, we were to begin a network, which was a momentous undertaking. Besides that, these things normally cost millions of dollars to begin, and we didn't have any money whatsoever.

I remember that after the discussion that day, I stayed behind in the boardroom. When alone, I said to the Lord, "So, this is what You want me to do?"

It was.

THE WAY THE LORD WORKS

A few days later, our television director related to my secretary that there was a Spanish network in Houston, Texas that wanted our Spanish programming. At any rate, she mentioned to them that we were starting a network. The man said, "Well, you need to see …" and he called the name of an organization. (We found later that it was the only one in the States that specializes in network programming.)

When we say network programming, we mean television that airs 24 hours a day, seven days a week. I suppose the reason there aren't more networks is that it's very difficult to program something on a constant, never-ending basis. But we had the means for the programming—we had the church, some of the best music in the world, and the preachers.

We called the people in question, and they told us that they would be here in Baton Rouge a couple of days later. When we told them what we were going to do, their answer was, "Reverend Swaggart, there aren't many cables left."

I looked at them and said, "Irrespective, do the best you can." I had no knowledge of what I was talking about, but the Holy Spirit was working.

About that time, one of the marketing channels over nationwide television went bankrupt, and that freed up many channels all over the nation. We were able to get quite a few of those channels.

THE FINANCES

As I have stated, we had no money, and yet, I was starting a network. When the Lord is in something, it works. People may wonder how it works, but it works.

If I remember correctly, we were on two cable systems, which were small, and Dish Television for several hours a day. That was the extent of our coverage.

I had told the Lord that we needed a million dollars to get started. To be frank, I wondered what the Lord would do. He had told me, "I'm going to open that door wide," and I knew that it extended to the finances.

We were in Costa Rica for a series of meetings when we received word of an opportunity to go on DirecTV full-time. This would take the SonLife Broadcasting Network nationwide, and we couldn't pass it up. The problem was, we had no money to pay for the channel. Adding DirecTV to our existing coverage, would push our broadcasting budget over $1 million a month. Even so, we stepped out in faith and signed the contract that day in Costa Rica and sent it back.

We went on the air that morning, telling the people what the Lord had called us to do, and I remember at about 3 o'clock in the afternoon of that particular day, there was a shout that went up from the phone people. I found out in a moment's time that we had just passed the $1 million mark. What a mighty God we serve!

As I dictate these notes, we are now in 90 million homes in the United States, and I expect the Lord to open up the balance of the television homes in this nation, which is 115 million. So, we have about 25 million to go. However, we are also in some 240 million homes outside of the United States because the Lord has told me to go through every door that He opens. That speaks of the whole world.

When we first went on, individuals asked who the preachers were that we were going to have on the network. The man with whom they were speaking said, "None."

They looked at him and said, "He won't last three months, if that." Their reasoning was, "How are they going to pay for it if they don't have other preachers on?"

Of course, we were going to pay for it as the Lord moved on the hearts of the people, which He did, which He has, and which He will continue to do.

On a worldwide basis, quite possibly, we go into more homes than any other television ministry in the world. Once again, we give the Lord the praise and the glory for this.

As with The Expositor's Study Bible, the Lord did not allow us to do this until the Message of the Cross was given to us, to make it a complete gospel. We constantly are receiving emails and phone calls telling us of lives changed and souls saved by the power of God as the Word of God, plus the moving and operation of the Holy Spirit, goes out over the television airwaves. Once again, we give the Lord all the credit and all the glory simply because He alone deserves all the praise and all the glory.

The Lord has given us some of the finest musicians and singers in the world. He has also given us preachers who have a depth of ministry that opens the Word of God to a greater degree than most have ever known. This is the Lord's doing, and it is marvelous in His eyes. As well, the Lord is using the network to proclaim the Message of the Cross to the world, with a moving of the Holy Spirit that is going to bring millions,

I believe, into the kingdom of God. As well, hundreds of thousands, if not millions, will be baptized with the Holy Spirit. In other words, I believe what we are about to see is going to be the greatest move of God the world has ever known.

I believe the Lord has told me this.

We are looking for His coming, in the clouds of heaven,
Coming back to earth to catch away His own,
Then may we all be ready, when the midnight cry is given,
To go and reign with Christ on His throne.

We're longing for the glory that awaits the faithful,
Who shall overcome, and every conflict win,
Press ever bravely onward, the prize is life eternal,
To all who win the fight over sin.

We're praying for the advent of our blessed Saviour,
Who has promised life to all who trust His grace;
His coming now is pending, the message being given,
And soon we'll see our Lord face to face.

We see the signs appearing of His blessed coming,
Lo, behold the fig leaves now becoming green;
The gospel of His kingdom, has gone to every nation,
That we are near the end can be seen.

Gladly, may we herald the message of His blessed appearing,
Soon He's coming in glory, tell to one and all,
Then awake ye saints of the Lord,
Why slumber when the end is nearing,
But get ready for the final call.

AMAZING GRACE

CHAPTER 22

FAMILY

"Our entire family serves
the Lord, and that's the
thing that really counts."

FAMILY

THE LORD WAS GRACIOUS and kind enough to me to have me cross the path of a tremendous man of God, A. N. Trotter, who left a marked influence on my life and ministry—an influence for the good. I saw the Holy Spirit in his life as I had never seen it in anyone else's. I saw and sensed the anointing of the Spirit upon his ministry as I had not witnessed previously.

While I had the privilege of preaching several campmeetings with Brother Trotter, by and large, I was not around him a great deal, and what I did learn, I learned mostly through his tapes. I saw in his life that which I wanted. I saw in his ministry that which I strongly desired. He charted the course, and I did my best to try to follow.

If the Lord tarries and ultimately takes me home to glory, likewise, I want to leave a mantle of power and the anointing of the Spirit that can be taken up by my son, my grandson, and as many as possible of the other preachers of the gospel over whom I might have even a modicum of influence.

As it concerns Donnie and Gabriel, the first reaction regarding my statements would be that I am prejudiced. While that is certainly possible, I have tried my best to go beyond prejudice and see the situation as it actually is.

I feel that my son, Donnie, and my grandson, Gabriel, are two of the greatest preachers in the world today. I realize that's quite a statement, but I honestly believe it to be true. They preach the Word, and they do so under the anointing of the Holy Spirit.

DONNIE

Donnie did not begin to preach until he was about 35 years old. Today, he probably preaches to more people than any other preacher in the world. I realize that's quite a statement, and, of course, the same would go for Gabriel; however, you must understand that all of the services at Family Worship Center are televised to go all over the world, which they do. That means that both of them are some of the most influential individuals in the world today, meaning that they are influencing millions for the cause of Christ, which is done by the gospel of Jesus Christ.

I personally do not think that the Lord could give Frances and me anything greater than to have a son and grandson occupy such a position for the cause of Christ. There could be nothing greater than that, and, of course, we give the Lord all the praise and all the glory.

When we were traveling in evangelistic work, which we did for many years, Donnie attended the school wherever it was that we were conducting a meeting. Actually, he attended some 32 schools before he entered high school in Baton Rouge, where he finished. He then attended Southwestern Bible College for a period of time. When he left Bible college and came back home to Baton Rouge, he went to work in the ministry, carrying out the most mundane tasks. So, I think I can say without any fear of contradiction that he has carried forth every single task that could be carried forth in the ministry, all the way from cleaning the restrooms to shipping out tapes and books, etc. In fact, the ministry is all that he has ever known all of his life.

Over 20 years ago, the Lord gave Donnie a powerful anointing to pray for believers to be baptized with the Holy Spirit. From that time until now, he has seen literally tens of thousands filled with the Holy Spirit all over the world. That is in conjunction with untold thousands having given their hearts and lives to the Lord Jesus Christ. The messages that he and Gabriel preach literally touch the church all over the world, and as previously stated, are, consequently, tremendously influential as it regards the cause of Christ.

THE GRANDCHILDREN

It's easy to see how that Donnie and Debbie raised Jennifer, Gabriel, and Matthew right. They were raised to love God and to do everything they can for His service in His work. Both Frances and I are so very, very proud of all three of them.

Our oldest grandchild, Jennifer, lives in Georgia with her husband, Cliff, and their two children, Harper, and Harrison. Jennifer has a bachelor's in elementary education from Oral Roberts University, and a master's of arts in early childhood education from Piedmont College. She's been working part-time as it regards the children of our church and also Family Christian Academy, as part of her degree is in this capacity.

Gabriel and Jill live here in Baton Rouge with their three daughters: Samantha, who is the oldest; Abby, and Caroline. Gabriel is one of the associate pastors here at Family Worship Center, and he's doing a phenomenal job. He is also preparing to head up our Bible college in its entirety.

Matthew lives in Oklahoma with his wife, Joanna, and their three children: Ryder, Lola, and Navy. Matthew has a bachelor's degree in graphic design from Oral Roberts University, and he uses his talents to design many of the graphics that you see over our television programming. He's been doing this for several years now, and he does an excellent job. He also has his own successful business.

The thing that is beautiful to me is that Jennifer, Gabriel and Matthew love the Lord with all of their hearts, and they do a gracious work for the Lord in their own ways. Yes, I would rather have all of them and their families in Baton Rouge, but at the same time, their talents are put to excellent use for which we thank the Lord. Their grandmother and I could not be more proud of them. As well, our great-grandkids are very, very special to Frances and me.

In fact, our entire family serves the Lord, and that's the thing that really counts. In other words, they love the Lord with all of their hearts, and that is the greatest blessing any father or grandfather could receive.

Tell me the story of Jesus,
Write on my heart every word;
Tell me the story most precious,
Sweetest that ever was heard.
Tell how the angels, in chorus,
Sang as they welcomed His birth,
"Glory to God in the highest!
Peace and good tidings to earth."

Fasting alone in the desert,
Tell of the days that are past,
How for our sins He was tempted,
Yet was triumphant at last.
Tell of the years of His labor,
Tell of the sorrow He bore,
He was despised and afflicted,
Homeless, rejected and poor.

Tell of the Cross where they nailed Him,
Writhing in anguish and pain;
Tell of the grave where they laid Him,
Tell how He liveth again.
Love in that story so tender,
Clearer than ever I see:
Stay, let me weep while you whisper,
"Love paid the ransom for me."

AMAZING GRACE

CHAPTER 23

A WORD FROM
THE LORD

"It was a dream given to a heathen monarch 3,700 years ago, and now it is about to come to pass."

A WORD FROM THE LORD

IT WAS 2010, not very long after the Lord had spoken to me about Him opening the door wide. It was early Sunday morning, and I was to minister at Family Worship Center that morning. I had awakened, and it was probably between 2 and 3 a.m. The Lord began to speak to my heart about the dream that Pharaoh had some 3,700 years ago, which was interpreted by Joseph. It's one of the most remarkable incidents in the entirety of the Word of God, which I think most would agree.

The dream given by the Lord to Pharaoh, which, as we have stated, was interpreted by Joseph, came in two parts.

THE FIRST PART

"And it came to pass at the end of two full years, that Pharaoh dreamed: and, behold, he stood by the river. And, behold, there came up out of the river seven well favored cattle and fatfleshed; and they

fed in a meadow. And, behold, seven other cattle came up after them out of the river, ill favored and leanfleshed; and stood by the other cattle upon the brink of the river. And the ill favored and leanfleshed cattle did eat up the seven well favored and fat cattle. So Pharaoh awoke" (Gen. 41:1-4).

THE SECOND DREAM

"And he slept and dreamed the second time: and, behold, seven ears of corn came up upon one stalk, rank and good. And, behold, seven thin ears and blasted with the east wind sprung up after them. And the seven thin ears devoured the seven rank and full ears. And Pharaoh awoke, and, behold, it was a dream" (Gen. 41:5-7).

THE INTERPRETATION

Joseph's interpretation, as given to him by the Holy Spirit, is as follows:

And Joseph said unto Pharaoh, The dream of Pharaoh is one: God has shown Pharaoh what He is about to do. The seven good cattle are seven years; and the seven good ears are seven years: the dream is one. And the seven thin and ill favored cattle that came up after them are seven years; and the seven empty ears blasted with the east wind shall be seven years of famine. This is the thing which I have spoken unto Pharaoh: What God is about to do He shows unto Pharaoh. Behold, there come seven years of great plenty throughout all the land of Egypt: And there shall arise after them seven years of famine; and all the plenty shall be forgotten in the land of Egypt; and the famine shall consume the land; And the plenty shall not be known in the land by reason of that famine following; for it shall be very grievous. And for that the dream was doubled unto Pharaoh twice; it is because the thing is established by God, and God will shortly bring it to pass (Gen. 41:25-32).

While Joseph alluded to the second dream, he never really explained it, except to say that it was very similar to the first dream, which it was.

There were two dreams, and the first one was fulfilled exactly as the Holy Spirit predicted. There were seven years of plenty in Egypt, with crops such as the nation had never seen before in its history. Then, there were seven years of famine, which were worse than anything Egypt or the East had ever seen before.

As stated, Joseph alluded to the second dream, but that was all. The emphasis was on the first dream of Pharaoh. It addressed Pharaoh's day and time, with Joseph being advanced to the most powerful man in the kingdom, other than Pharaoh himself—a dream which did shortly come to pass, and it lasted for some 14 years.

INTERPRETATION OF THE SECOND DREAM

I believe the Lord has told me several things about this second dream of Pharaoh. They are:

- The second dream has not yet been fulfilled but is on the very eve of coming to pass exactly as the Lord gave it to the monarch some 3,700 years ago.

- The seven healthy ears that came up on the stalk represent a move of God that is about to take place, which will result in hundreds of thousands, if not millions, being swept into the kingdom of God. In a sense, it is the same as the first dream, as far as the great harvest was concerned, which was the greatest Egypt had ever known. If I am correct in what I am saying, this, as well, will be the greatest harvest—not of grain, but of souls—that the world or the church has ever known.

- The seven ears that were and rotten represent the seven years of great tribulation that's coming upon this planet. It will be worse than the world has ever seen before, according to the words of our Lord (Mat. 24:21).

- If that is the case, then the seven healthy buds, fatfleshed and vibrant, represent a harvest of souls. As the seven fat cattle represented a harvest such as Egypt had never seen previously, likewise, the seven fatfleshed buds represent the greatest harvest of souls the world has ever known.

- I believe the Lord also told me that this would be the last great move before the coming great tribulation.

- As well, this ministry—Jimmy Swaggart Ministries— will play a part in this harvest.

If all of this is correct, then we are very close to coming to fulfillment—*very close.* I do not believe that the Lord is going to come back for a sick church and that alone. While this age speaks of apostasy—and great apostasy at that—still, the Lord will not be denied. He never diminishes but always advances with a greater move than ever.

While I do not see revival at this time, but rather apostasy, I do see a harvest. Such a harvest can be brought about now due to television, when it could not have been brought about a hundred years ago. It sobers one to grasp the fact that God spoke to a heathen monarch, who didn't even know that the Lord existed, and gave him information that would be fulfilled shortly, and that which has not yet been fulfilled, but which is on the very eve of fulfillment.

The Holy Spirit did not have Joseph to interpret this second dream because it remained for the far distant future. Once again, I will say that if I am right in that which I have said, then we are very, very close to all of these tremendous things being fulfilled. In other words, the rapture of the church has to be very, very close, after which, the world will be plunged into tribulation as never before.

In the great meetings in the 1980s, the Lord gave this ministry the privilege of seeing the greatest harvest of souls the world had ever known. How I thank God for that.

As well, we saw the greatest number of believers baptized with the Holy Spirit with the evidence of speaking with other tongues that the world has ever known.

Then, the Lord gave us the help to develop The Expositor's Study Bible, which I believe is the Bible that the Holy Spirit is using for the 21st century and, one might say, for the end of all things.

And then, the Lord has given us the honor and the privilege of establishing the SonLife Broadcasting Network, which is presently touching the world, and which I believe the Lord will use in this latter day harvest.

We give the Lord all the praise and all the glory for this, for without Him, nothing can be done.

I look and see earth's golden riches,
The hoarding mob, for selfish gain;
The toil of hands for ease and comfort,
I look again and see earth's golden falling grain.

It's harvest time, harvest time,
The Saviour's calling, the grain is falling.
Do not wait; it's growing late,
Behold, the fields are white; it's harvest time.

EPILOGUE

GOD CALLED ME FOR world evangelism when I was a 9-year-old child. Of course, my understanding at that time was limited, but still, even from that moment, I had a general idea as to what my ministry would be and what it would do. So, whenever the Lord helped us respecting television and giant citywide crusades in certain parts of the world, with literally tens of thousands responding to an invitation to accept Christ, this was not a surprise to me. In my spirit I had known it all along.

However, with this call, the Lord gave me a special faith, or, in other words, the gift of faith, enabling me to believe that I would be able to reach a great part of this world with the gospel. Countless times, I've had other preachers to ridicule me about this very thing, insinuating that it was impossible to believe God for the entirety of the world, or at least reaching them with the gospel.

However, what seemed impossible to them—and in fact was impossible—was not impossible at all to me. I believed it for the simple reason that God had called me for this purpose and had given me the faith to believe for this, despite the fact that it was of such magnitude.

As a result, the Lord has helped us to see hundreds of thousands of people brought to a saving knowledge of Jesus Christ. He has helped us to see tens of thousands baptized with the Holy Spirit. He has helped us to see untold thousands delivered by the mighty power of God from the worst types of bondage with which Satan imprisons people. Without this special faith, it would not have been possible for these things to have been brought about.

At this present time, the SonLife Broadcasting Network is reaching out to the entirety of the world. This is gospel television 24 hours a day, seven days a week. What we are seeing now is phenomenal, however, I believe what is being given to us at the present constitutes only mercy drops round us falling, by comparison to what the Lord is going to do in the very near future. I believe we are going to see a harvest of souls such as the world has never seen before, and as well, believers by the tens of thousands, even by the hundreds of thousands, baptized with the Holy Spirit with the evidence of speaking with other tongues.

I mentioned this earlier in this volume, but it bears repeating here. The Lord gave me a dream when I was about 10 years old—a dream that I little understood at the time, but have come to understand its meaning presently. I dreamed I was standing outside in front of our house up in northeast Louisiana. I looked to my right, and there was a sphere or globe of this planet literally suspended in space, approximately 10 feet high and maybe 10 feet from me. For some reason or the other, it did not seem strange to me in the dream for the globe to be suspended in space, and if I remember correctly, it was slowly turning, and was in color. I knew it was a globe of this planet, because the continents were visible.

All of a sudden, there stood a figure that was right beside it, actually looking up at it. Instantly, I knew that it was Satan. But again, his presence did not seem to scare me. I said nothing to him, and he said nothing to me at the outset. He looked up at the globe and stared at it for a period of time, and then turned and looked at me and said, "You will not do it; I will stop you."

He then turned back, looking at the globe again, and then turned back to me and said the same identical thing again: "You will not do it; I will stop you."

At that time, I did not understand what he meant. Now I do know. He was speaking of world evangelism—the call that God has given me. And yes, he has done everything within his power to stop us. And to be sure, I blame myself for his successes.

THE VISION OF THE BURNING OF THE CHAFF

I believe it was in 1982, in Guatemala City, Guatemala, during a crusade, when the Lord gave me a vision concerning the sifting of the wheat and, more particularly, the burning of the chaff. It was sometime after midnight, and I had arisen to go into the adjoining room to pray about the coming meeting and other things.

As the Lord brought this vision of the threshing floor before my eyes, I plainly saw the chaff completely separated from the wheat as it piled up somewhat on the ground around the threshing floor. As well, I saw the flames hungrily lick at the chaff and burning it, exactly as described in Matthew 3:12: *"Whose fan is in his hand, and he will throughly purge his floor, and gather his wheat into the garner; but he will burn up the chaff with unquenchable fire."*

As the Spirit of God moved upon me mightily that night, and with the vision of the burning chaff in stark relief before my eyes, I asked the Lord as to the necessity of the burning of this refuse, especially considering that it had been fully separated from the wheat and was not actually even on the threshing floor any longer.

NO TRACE LEFT

The Lord answered me in beautiful simplicity by saying, "There must be no trace left of the flesh, of which the chaff is a type."

At that particular time, little did I realize exactly what that vision meant and how it would pertain to me personally.

As with Job and Peter (and no doubt millions of others) I felt the terrible pain—although an absolute necessity—of the burning of the chaff with unquenchable fire. But yet, it has served to draw me closer to God than I have ever been in my life.

In the spring of 1988, with my ministry in pieces, with a thousand questions unanswered, and with my name a joke over the entirety of the world, I remember awaking early one morning before daylight, that is, if I had ever been to sleep, and asking the Lord why such had to be, and more particularly, why in this manner.

Public humiliation is of such portent that most do not survive it, especially on a worldwide scale. Actually, without the grace of God, I don't think such would be survivable.

Realizing that Job's friends are abundant—and with their recriminations they seem to have all the answers—but to those few who truly know God, the answers, if any at all, are not that simple.

That early morning hour, as the hot tears burned my cheeks, and when death would have seemed pleasant, the Lord, I believe, gently spoke to me.

He said, "You have asked Me why, and I will answer you in this manner: As I crippled Jacob, I had to cripple you, and whatever I do with you in the future, you will always be reminded by the limp."

What the Lord gave us in the 1980s was absolutely miraculous, with the greatest harvest of souls that had ever been witnessed or experienced, and for which we give God all the praise and all the glory. But I feel the best is yet to come. I believe we are going to see even a greater harvest, and that was what the Lord spoke to my heart in 2010.

And as well, anytime that the Lord calls one to do something, He imparts the necessary faith—the gift of faith—in order for this work to be carried out. And, by the grace of God, it will be done.

I love to tell the story
Of unseen things above,
Of Jesus and His glory,
Of Jesus and His love.

I love to tell the story,
Because I know it's true;
It satisfies my longings
As nothing else can do.

ABOUT EVANGELIST JIMMY SWAGGART

The Rev. Jimmy Swaggart is a Pentecostal evangelist whose anointed preaching and teaching has drawn multitudes to the Cross of Christ since 1955.

As an author, he has written more than 50 books, commentaries, study guides, and The Expositor's Study Bible, which has sold more than 3.2 million copies.

As an award-winning musician and singer, Brother Swaggart has recorded more than 50 gospel albums and sold nearly 17 million recordings worldwide.

For more than six decades, Brother Swaggart has channeled his preaching and music ministry through multiple media venues including print, radio, television and the Internet.

In 2010, Jimmy Swaggart Ministries launched its own cable channel, SonLife Broadcasting Network, which airs 24 hours a day to a potential viewing audience of more than 2 billion people around the globe.

Brother Swaggart also pastors Family Worship Center in Baton Rouge, Louisiana, the church home and headquarters of Jimmy Swaggart Ministries.

Jimmy Swaggart Ministries materials can be found at **www.jsm.org**.

the Jimmy Swaggart Crusade
Experience the Difference for Yourself
Birmingham Crusade
March 21-23, 1986
Friday & Saturday, 7:30 P.M.
Sunday, 3:30 P.M.
CRUSADE
HOTEL
JIMMY SWAGGART BIBLE COLLEGE